101 THEATRE GAMES

DEDICATED TO THE CHILD SPIRIT IN EVERYONE

Written by Mila Johansen

Published by Classics With A Twist
in association with
PLAYERS PRESS, Inc.

101 THEATRE GAMES

Classics With A Twist
in association with
PLAYERS PRESS, Inc.

Library of Congress Cataloging-in-Publication Data

Johansen, Mila, 1954-
101 theatre games : dedicated to the child spirit in everyone / by Mila Johansen.
p.   cm.
ISBN 0-88734-911-0
1. Acting--Study and teaching.   2. Children as actors.   I. Title.   II. Title : One hundred one theatre games.   III. Title : One hundred and one theatre games.
PN3157.J57   1994
792'.028'07--dc20   94-25070
                                                                CIP

Simultaneously Published
U.S.A., U.K., Canada and Australia

Printed in the U.S.A.

TABLE OF CONTENTS

TABLE OF CONTENTS - Cont'd

MORE GAMES

TABLE OF CONTENTS - Cont'd

TABLE OF CONTENTS - Cont'd

101 THEATRE GAMES
INTRODUCTION

This book is designed for both the classroom teacher and the drama teacher. These games are also designed for any director to use in a rehearsal situation.

These games have been carefully developed over the past seven years in a highly successful drama program. Games are an excellent way to teach acting skills and techniques. The concept is that once a participant, whether a child or an adult, plays a game, he or she will never forget the skill or technique employed for that game.

These games are valuable to the classroom teacher for imparting techniques that can be used in everyday life; especially techniques that teach students how to get along and work with others. Any teacher, anywhere, can open this book and within ten minutes have his or her students playing a theatre game.

These games will bring out the innate talent that is in everyone. Everyone does have talent. It's just that some people know how to use it and some don't. Some people have had a chance to use it and some haven't. Some people will take longer to develop than others and that's okay. Some people are ready to perform today and some are not. Some people will never be ready and that's okay. We are all at different stages of fulfilling our full talent-potential. We all need the opportunity to explore and develop our natural abilities. Playing games puts everyone on the same footing and allows everyone to try things at a comfortable level of involvement. What is important here is the process, not the outcome. The process of developing talent doesn't end today, or at the end of a production, or at the end of a school year. It is a lifetime process that the teacher or director will influence. A good director or teacher recognizes that everyone has a gift to offer. Finding a way to use each person's special talent is the mark of a teacher or director who understands the developmental process.

This book can be used in many different ways. A teacher may want to open up the book to a random page and take potluck. A popular activity is to let a student open the book to a page, picking the game that will be played that day. Or, starting at the beginning and systematically going through from beginning to end, a teacher can build techniques which create a solid foundation. In a continuing drama class, the latter choice would be preferable for more serious study.

Many of these theatre games can be used as a daily warm-up for either the classroom setting or as a warm-up before starting play practice. The freeze-walk is especially good as a warm-up. It gives the students a chance to perform without being watched, and an opportunity to learn from each other as they relate to one another. It is also an activity that they can look forward to, providing them with a loose structure where anything can happen!

Many of these exercises send the participants off into small groups of 2-5 to create their own skits and pieces. It is important that the coach give constructive criticism at the end of each performance whether a short skit or larger production. These should include ideas and suggestions that students can learn from that will help them to improve upon the piece. Time permitting, send them off to work on it using the suggestions to make it better to perform again.

It is extremely important to create a good audience atmosphere among the participants. There should be absolutely no talking, whispering, feet shuffling, or noise of any kind. It is important for every actor/actress to be a good listener and a good audience. Each participant should think about how he or she wants the audience to act during their own performance and give the same respect to the other performers. Watching others and listening to others is one of the best ways to get ideas and to learn.

Many of these exercises can be and have been incorporated into two hour or full day workshops for schools, drama groups and various other organizations.

Following is a page of key words that are commonly used in the theatre world. Key words may be used to keep the correct focus on the activity for both the participants and the teacher. You may want to add a few key words yourself.

KEY WORDS

This is a list of key words that every teacher, director, and group leader should know or have in mind when leading these games and exercises. These are key words for anyone who is participating in the theatre process on any level. You may want to memorize them. Use them often.

Instinct	Vulnerability
Focus	Truth
Risk	Breath
React	Believe
Relax	Energy
Spontaneous	Teamwork
Timing	Active listening
Enunciate	Project
Communicate	Body Language
Understand	Think fast
Convincing	Freeze
Concentrate	Exaggerate
Creativity	Dare
Don't think	Use your space
Use past memories	Be a good audience

FILL IN THE BLANKS

    Following is a list of important sentences that can help teach theatre etiquette and techniques. Test your group and see how many of these they already know. Ask participants to memorize these sentences. Start saying these sentences to the group, leaving out the underlined words. Let the group fill in the blanks verbally. These thirty-one sentences are great brain teasers.

1. There are no small parts, only small _____. (actors)
2. Listen to the _____. (director)
3. Never argue with the _____. (director)
4. Don't direct _____. (others)
5. Always be on _____. (time)
6. Always bring your _____ to every rehearsal. (script)
7. Don't chew _____. (gum)
8. Practice, Practice, _____! (practice)
9. Memorize your lines, ___ _____ __ _____. (as soon as possible)
10. Memorize your _____ lines. (cue)
11. Memorize the scene _____. (order)
12. Practice still makes _____. (perfect)
13. Maintain a positive _____ at all times. (attitude)
14. Create movements to go with the _____. (words)
15. Research your _____. (character)
16. If you don't know the meaning of a word or a phrase, _____ ___ ___. (look it up.)
17. Facial expressions are called _____. (mugs)
18. Enunciate e-ver-y _____. (word)
19. If you or someone else forgets, _____. (improvise)
20. When you are not speaking, you are _____. (listening)
21. Practice active _____. (listening)
22. If you can see the audience, _____ _____ _____ _____. (they can see you)
23. Absolutely no talking or whispering _____. (backstage)
24. Keep your feet _____. (quiet)
25. Never turn your back to the audience, unless the _____ tells you to. (director)
26. Before you perform, _____. (warm-up)
27. Don't complain about your _____. (costume)
28. Don't complain about _____. (anything)
29. Never, never, say anything about another person unless it's _____. (positive)
30. Don't forget to _____. (breathe)
31. You perform unless you're _____. (dead)

4

FILL IN THE BLANKS

Following are the thirty-one sentences printed without the answers.

1. There are no small parts, only small _____.
2. Listen to the _____.
3. Never argue with the _____.
4. Don't direct _____.
5. Always be on _____.
6. Always bring your _____ to every rehearsal.
7. Don't chew _____.
8. Practice, Practice, _____!
9. Memorize your lines, ___ _____ __ _____.
10. Memorize your _____ lines.
11. Memorize the scene _____.
12. Practice still makes _____.
13. Maintain a positive _____ at all times.
14. Create movements to go with the _____.
15. Research your _____.
16. If you don't know the meaning of a word or a phrase, _____ __ __.
17. Facial expressions are called _____.
18. Enunciate e-ver-y _____.
19. If you or someone else forgets, _____.
20. When you are not speaking, you are _____.
21. Practice active _____.
22. If you can see the audience, _____ _____ _____ _____.
23. Absolutely no talking or whispering _____.
24. Keep your feet _____.
25. Never turn your back to the audience, unless the _____ tells you to.
26. Before you perform, _____.
27. Don't complain about your _____.
28. Don't complain about _____.
29. Never, never, say anything about another person unless it's _____.
30. Don't forget to _____.
31. You perform unless you're _____.

INTRODUCTION TO WARM - UPS

Warm-ups may be one of the singularly most important parts of learning the theatre craft. Warm-ups are a wonderful way to expose students and performers to the basics. For some, it is a way to keep toned, a reminder of things they already know. Following is a group of specific warm-ups. One of the best warm-ups to use as a standard starting technique is the "Freeze-walk" on the next page. It is a versatile format in which you can easily incorporate any aspect that you think needs work.

It is suggested that performance groups start these warm-ups in rehearsals so the group is used to doing them. I have found over and over that warm-ups are so much more effective if they are used throughout the rehearsal process. Besides bringing the group together in a team spirit, they provide strategies for smoothing out a lot of the rough edges in each actor/actress.

It is also vital that all performers develop good warm-up techniques within themselves. The warm-ups done in a group should only be a small part of an actor's/actress' warm-up regime. Because of time restraints, the warm-ups done in a group usually just skim the surface and are primarily done to create team spirit and support. One of the most important things a drama teacher can teach students is the importance of warming up. In many performance situations there is little or no time set aside for warm-ups. The difference between warming up and not warming up, for most actors and actresses, can be the difference between having a good performance and having a great performance.

THE FREEZE-WALK

This exercise is the mainstay of my teaching technique. It is my own personal point of departure. I can take any group to any depth or height with this game. This is my most powerful technique builder. This is my secret weapon against ignorance in theatre. With this, I can tear down any blocks or barriers that stand in the way. I can strip anyone of theatre ignorance single-handedly. This is "How the west was won". Once a person plays a game, he or she will never forget the winning strategy.

Every game in this book is vitally important to the whole process of becoming an actor, of becoming a whole person, and this game is where we begin. As you will see, this simple set of rules can take on many dimensions and accomplish a lot in a short period of time. I use it in workshop situations and as a warm-up at every rehearsal. No matter what else I have on my agenda for the day, I start with at least ten minutes of the freeze-walk. I focus on what I think the group needs to work on. I have written these rules as I say them in my workshop.

THE RULES:
1) **We are going to see who can take direction. When I say walk, walk.**
2) **When I say freeze, freeze! Freeze immediately! Freeze tight like ice or like a statue, don't move a muscle. Don't think, don't blink. If you think you are going to blink, look down.**
3) **If you are in a precarious position and are going to fall, make it one movement and freeze immediately.**
4) **This is mime. Don't make a sound. Don't let us hear your feet. Don't even let us hear your breath.**
5) **I am going to tell you to do all sorts of things. Learn to take direction, do exactly as I say, even if I tell you to stand on your head or to do a tap dance. Don't say a word, just do it.**

(You will need to remind the group of the rules, often, throughout the exercise.)

I have played this game with both children and adults for years. It is an easy way to involve everyone within ten minutes in a non-threatening manner. It is a great way to build instant rapport between director/teacher and participant. It gives you a working format that you can continue from day to day. It is also an instant barrier buster for anyone doing a one day workshop. It puts everyone on the same footing and bonds the group together as one unit.

In the next few games that follow, I am going to "say it" exactly as I say it in a workshop or rehearsal situation. You may want to imitate my lingo at first until you develop your own. You may even want to read these exercises until you get a feeling for the whole concept. This is my style of coaching and you will inevitably develop your own style and format.

One thing you will want to learn is, how to switch from one activity to another without skipping a beat. It is important never to lose your group for even a minute. It is especially difficult in a large group to get and keep the attention of all participants. It is important to learn how long to continue one activity and when to switch to a new activity. You always have to be thinking ahead. Before you finish one activity, already know in your mind what the next one is and say it in the last few seconds of the previous activity. This way you continue the flow from point A to point P and keep the atmosphere fresh. When I first started teaching, I made a list of games that I could refer to. I rarely needed to look at the list, but it was there if I needed it. I always listed more games than I could use and therefore, never ran out of ideas.

The Basic Freeze-Walk/Learning To Walk | 1

I start by letting the participants define the art of miming. This establishes it in the minds of those who have no previous experience in mime and reminds everyone else of the rules. Establish a physical perimeter in which the participants stay throughout the freeze-walk. Use the stage or define a section of the room and ask them to stay within those boundaries. The whole idea of the freeze-walk is to set up scenarios and let the participants act them out in mime. Between scenarios you will be calling out, "freeze". This way you are alternating an activity with a freeze. You can control the situation with the freezes. If it is getting too loud or out of hand for any reason, call out freeze and have them hold it while you talk. Let them get used to holding their freezes for some length of time. Sometimes you will want to set up the next activity while they are frozen, listening to you. The following is only an example. You will want to make up your own instances and situations. This game will grow on you. It is an evolving process for both the director/teacher and the participants.

"Who can tell what mime is? (Someone will volunteer.) That's right! It is acting without sound. No talking, no sighing, no bodily noise, no sound. Okay. Who can show us what I mean when I say 'freeze'? (Someone will volunteer.) Good, now see how Justin is completely frozen. He won't even blink. That is exactly what I want when I say 'freeze'. Everything we do in the next twenty minutes will be done with no sound. When I say 'freeze', I want everyone to stop immediately and freeze in whatever position I catch you in. Alright, everybody walk. Just walk. Nothing else. Walk slowly with your head down. Don't look up and don't touch anybody. You can feel where the other people are; use your radar. We all have radar, just like bats. We have to learn to use it."

You are walking by yourself. Get into your own space. Get comfortable. Just walk, don't think. Freeze. Don't move, don't blink, don't even think, just freeze. Look down if you think you're going to blink. Now walk a little faster, keep your head down. Don't think, just be in your own space, just be with yourself. Keep your feet quiet. Freeze. Don't move. (Walk through the group looking at each person so that they know you see them.) I'm going to walk through you and I don't want you to move at all. Freeze like ice. Don't look at me. Look down if you think you are going to blink. Stay frozen until I say to move. Now, look at the ceiling, use your radar, don't touch anyone. Keep walking, looking at the ceiling. Walk a little faster. Freeze. Freeze tight. Amy stay frozen, don't move a muscle. Everyone else come over and see how tight Amy is frozen. Don't touch her. She's good at this. Now everyone, look straight ahead and walk as fast as you can without touching anyone. Don't run, walk fast, faster, faster."

You are on the streets of New York City and you are late for a meeting or you're late for work and might get fired. You don't want to touch anybody because you don't know who they are. They are all strangers. Walk faster, you're late! This is the third time you've been late this week and you are afraid of getting fired. You are agitated and the other people on the sidewalk are in your way. Move around them. Faster, faster! Freeze! Don't you dare move. Spencer, stay frozen, do not move. Everyone else come look at his interesting position and how frozen he is.

(Go through a series of showing off people who can hold a pose. Pick people with interesting positions giving the rest of the group ideas through example.) Everyone walk as fast as you can without running. You are extremely late, look at your watch. You are carrying a briefcase in one hand and looking at your watch on the other. Don't touch anyone! Faster, faster, oh, no, you dropped your briefcase and all your papers have flown out all over the sidewalk. Stoop down and pick them up, put them back into your briefcase. Close the briefcase and continue on. Now you're even later than before. Faster, faster. Stop and think. Oh, my goodness, today is Saturday, you don't work on Saturday. Oh, what a relief! Still holding your briefcase in one hand, wipe your forehead with relief with the other hand. Start walking slowly, no noise. Hey, today is a beautiful day. Show me, by the way you are walking, what a beautiful day it is. It's one of those perfect spring days, not too warm, not too cool, just right. Show me. Freeze!"

The Basic Freeze-Walk ... continued

"Now you are all joggers, jogging down the street, feeling good, just jogging. Keep your feet quiet. (Anticipate any noise whether it is made by feet or talking and nip it in the bud.) You're starting to sweat and it is beginning to drip into your eyes. Your clothing is sticking to your body. You're getting hot! Keep jogging. Shake out your arms. Freeze! Don't move a muscle! Okay. Walk as fast as you can going in all different directions, do not touch anybody. Freeze! Walk again as fast as you can and when I say switch directions, turn as fast as you can and go the other way without bumping into anyone. Walk fast! Switch! (Let them walk a few steps) Switch! Switch! (Vary your timing on when you call out the word "Switch.") Faster! Switch! Don't touch anyone! Switch! Switch! Freeze!"

"Now everyone move in slow motion. I mean slow, as if you are caught in a vat of thick honey and your body is forced to move at a slow pace. Use your muscles to keep your body moving slowly. Slower, like a slow motion movie. Now take chances and use different levels, move around on the floor, up on your toes. Keep it in slow motion. Freeze! (Walk around and look at each person.) Okay. Continue in slow motion. Take risks and make your movements interesting. Freeze! Walk as fast as you can. Faster, faster! Don't run, do not touch anyone! Freeze! Now you are an elderly person. Show me old. Get into it. Keep going as I talk. Not all old people are hunched over as you all are now. Many older folks are healthy and exercise daily. Many older folks are in better shape than some of us. But for our uses, we need to use the cliche of old to create the difference from young. We are over exaggerating. You have a cane and your hand that is holding the cane is shaking. Get into it. Good, very good. Now stop and take the hanky out of your back pocket, remove your glasses and wipe your glasses with your hanky. Put your glasses back on and put your hanky back in your pocket. Continue your walk with your cane. Freeze! Now you are a child chewing gum and kicking a ball. You are having a good ol' time and thoroughly enjoying yourself. Oops, the ball has gotten away from you. Chase it down, pick it up and bounce it instead. You are still chewing gum. Bounce the ball higher and higher, watch it, catch it after each bounce and bounce it again. Freeze! Okay. Everybody go find a seat and we will begin our rehearsal."

That is only the tip of the iceberg. You can do anything in this exercise: tap dancing, ballet, football, any sport; you can explore any character. The following games are suggestions and ideas, directions for you to pursue. Keep reminding the group of the rules and guidelines. This helps them develop good habits.

Divide the group up into pairs and have them hold hands. If there is an extra person, let one group have three. No matter what you tell them to do they will hold hands at all times and never break apart. Don't worry, they will get used to holding hands. It is a fun game that everyone likes to play. It gives them the sense of working together and an understanding they just can't do anything they want; they are linked to someone else and they must make decisions together. There is absolutely no talking so they must learn to make decisions together in complete silence. This is an exercise in trust.

"No matter what, do not let go of your partner's hand. You must do everything together. I just want you to walk together. It is a nice day and you are feeling good. Now walk a little faster. Faster. Now, walk as fast as you can. Do not touch another group. Stay to yourselves. Faster! Freeze! Now you are a tourist in New York City and you are running from one site to another, pointing, getting excited. You want your partner to see everything. Run over there and show your partner the sight. Now the other person, run and point. Keep it up. Point and run. Look at it, take a picture of it, don't let go. Hold your partner's hand. Point and run. Freeze! Don't move. (Walk through looking to make sure that everyone is completely frozen.) Okay, now one of you is an elderly person and the other one is helping that person across the street. Go. Don't let go of your hands. If you're the one helping, you have to go as slowly as that person. Be patient. Be helpful. Freeze! You are both late and are in a big hurry. Walk as fast as you can without running and without touching any other pair. Faster! Faster! Turn and go the other way! Freeze! Walk, take turns telling secrets to each other. Re-act to one another. Don't really talk, just move your lips as if you are talking. Don't let us hear you. Listen to the person who is telling, then switch and the other person listen. Freeze! You are both blind. Close your eyes, hold on to one another and do not touch anyone else. Use your radar. Don't touch anyone except your partner. You are the blind leading the blind. (Give them time to explore.) Freeze!"

As you can see, you can go anywhere with this one. Be as creative as possible. Come up with as many instances as you can think of. Switch pairs around often.

Write Your Own Script For Freeze-Walking In Pairs

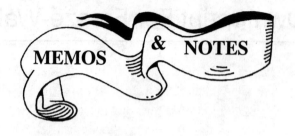

MEMOS & NOTES

Freeze-Walk With Emotions | 3

This is a great way to develop characterized walking. Sometimes the best way to show a character is by the way he or she walks. Often it is our emotions that dictate how we walk. This gives everyone a good solid introduction to putting emotions on the face. It is somehow easier at first to combine emotions with another movement, hence, walking with emotions. Remind the group to keep absolute silence. No stomping around to show that we are angry. No heavy sighing to help us produce a particular emotion. We are on our own; we cannot use sound as a crutch. We must pull it out from deep within us; we must really feel that emotion.

Guide the participants through various emotions. Tell them to put that emotion on their faces and watch how that emotion makes them feel. Example: Sadness would make them hunch over with the weight of the world on their shoulders. Happiness would make them walk straight and tall with their chest out, etc. Say the emotion, elaborate on that emotion and the way it makes them feel, and when it looks like they really have it, call out "freeze". Tell them to freeze with that emotion on their faces. Walk around and take a look. Choose someone who epitomizes that emotion perfectly, tell him or her to remain frozen while everyone else comes over to take a look. Seeing their peers commit to the emotions will show participants how far they can go. Seeing each other's faces will stimulate more commitment to each emotion.

Animals On Parade | 4

There is nothing quite as explicit as playing an animal. It is a great opportunity for any actor or actress to sharpen physical movements. Most animals have specific moves that can be imitated. You can usually guess what animal a person is trying to be by seeing the movements. Yet it is important to find the exact moves that will get that particular animal across a stage. This freeze-walk is great for casts who will be playing animals or just as an exercise in imitating life.

Treat this exercise just like the previous freeze-walk exercises, but go through the animal kingdom.

Freeze-Walk In The Weather | 5

This exercise takes the participants through the various forms of weather. Again, this is only an example. Use these exact words or make up your own.

"You are walking and it is a perfect day. There is a delightful breeze and you can feel it all over your body. Show me what a nice day it is. There are little puffy clouds sailing by and you don't want this day to end. (Give them time to experience the day.) But now a single grey cloud is passing over your head and it begins to sprinkle gently. It feels good, not even enough to get your clothing wet. Oh, but what is this? A bigger cloud is directly over you and it is raining harder and you are beginning to get wet, in fact it is soaking through your clothing, you are getting really wet. Freeze! Now it is pouring and you want to find cover. Run and stand under that doorway over there, quick, get under it! You want to get to where you are going so you are going to run from doorway to doorway. Run! Quick, duck into the next doorway. Run! Duck! Run! Freeze! You are walking on a slippery, icy sidewalk. You are slipping all over the place but you don't fall down. It's dangerously slippery! Grab onto the post in front of you and pull yourself to it. Freeze! You are walking in hail, big pellets of hail that are nailing you on the head. They hurt! Ouch! Cover your head. That does some good but now they are hitting your arms hard. Freeze! It is hot. You are extremely hot. So hot that you can hardly move. You are lethargic. Hot. It's 110 degrees in the shade. You are sweaty and uncomfortable and it's going to be that way all day. There is nothing you can do about it. Hot. Freeze! That's right, you're freezing. It's icy cold out there. In fact, you're shivering and shaking. You're freezing cold. No noise, just show us how very cold you are. Freeze! We're at the beach. Stop and take a look at the waves. Good waves. Take your towel out of your satchel and lay it out. Sit on it and take a look around. The sun feels good. Take out your suntan lotion and spread it all over your body. You don't want to burn. Look at the waves once more. Now lay back and enjoy the sunshine. Freeze!"

Finding Clues to Your Character Through Walking | 6

This game is one that I developed for performing casts. I use it for character development. I systematically go through each character in the play or musical. I ask the person playing each character, one at a time, to move out of the group and stand with me. Then I ask the entire group to walk in the way they think that character would walk, to give the person who is now watching ideas. I usually point out a few people who are capturing just the right mannerisms and characteristics through their walk. It never fails to help the person playing that character to get plenty of ideas to use.

The primary goal of this exercise is to get the participants used to being on stage, to get them comfortable with just being looked at and to gain experience with eye to eye contact. It is an excellent first day exercise. In it's simplicity it accomplishes many things. It can be used often, developing in complexity.

Besides the Freeze-walk, this exercise requires the most coaching of any of the games. So, I have included a step-by-step example of what I mean when I say COACHING! You may write it out before class or make it up as you go along. This is simply the way I talk. You will of course have your own coaching style. Each group will be different, you will find your own level of control. Feel free to read this example until you come up with your own.

Half the class stands in one row downstage facing the audience while the other half sits in audience position. The teacher is the coach. Complete silence."We will look at you and you will look at us. No matter what I tell you to do, DO NOT take your eyes off of us, no matter what, we will look at you and you look at us. Just get comfortable with it and please remember that everything you are asked to do is in mime, no noise, no talking, no feet shuffling, no noise!" (Anticipate everything, uncomfortableness, wandering eyes, laughing, keep reminding them not to take their eyes off the audience and remind the audience to uphold complete silence.)

"Look into someone's eyes at all times, DO NOT MOVE, DO NOT MAKE A SOUND, just look at us and we'll look at you. (Pause, if you see any activity or hear any noise, comment.) Just get comfortable looking at us while we look at you. (Pause, let a long silence go by, this pause is the most valuable.) GOOD! GOOD! Now relax and get more comfortable looking at us. (Pause) Okay, everyone onstage. There is a piece of bubble gum in your mouth, let us see you chew it. NO Noise! DO NOT take your eyes off us! Keep chewing. (Pause) Now take the gum out of your mouth, split it in half and give one half to a person next to you. DON'T look at this person. DON'T laugh. Look at us. Squeeze the two pieces together and put it in your mouth and chew. Keep chewing."

"Keep looking at us. Now stand on one leg. (Pause) Keep chewing. No matter what I tell you to do, I want you to chew your gum for the rest of the exercise. You each have a bathroom mirror in front of you. Look into it. We are the mirror so look at us. Keep chewing. The mirror is dirty so you are going to wash it. Tear off a paper towel. Pick up your windex with the other hand; spray it and wash the mirror. Do a good job. (Pause) Okay, is it clean? Throw the paper towel in the trash can. Look at us. Put the windex down. Girls, put on make up and brush your hair. Boys, comb your hair and shave. Use your memory to do this. Girls, if you haven't ever put on make up before, remember someone doing it in a movie. Same thing with the boys, use your memory. It is your best resource. Think about the process, break it down. (Give them some time to get into it. Say whatever is needed to keep them going, give them ideas, mascara, eyeliner, shaving cream.) Keep chewing! Look at us! Don't drop things. Remember where you got them and return them to their proper place. Take your time, look at us. (It is important to remind them to look at the audience each time you change an activity.) Keep chewing! Okay, now keep looking at us as I call out an emotion. We want to see that emotion on your face. Remember that emotion, feel that emotion, and then let your face show us. Stop chewing. Take the gum out of your mouth and put it on the bottom of your shoe. Okay, the first emotion is ANGER! You are steaming mad, show it on your face. Look right into our eyes and show us how angry you are. (Pause) Now I want SADNESS, you are so sad, you feel like crying, but you don't (pause) but now the sadness is overwhelming and you must cry, NO NOISE, remember this is mime. Don't cover your face with your hands, you are crying. (Pause) Now you are just the opposite, you are HAPPY! Give me happiness on your face. More, you are excited, you have just received the most wonderful news in the WORLD, but now you are confused."

"Show me confusion. Look at us (Pause) UGGG!!! You just saw something disgusting like a giant squashed bug on the sidewalk. DON'T LOOK DOWN! Show me disgust on your face. Good, you all remember that one, don't you? One more emotion; show me anxiety, you are anxious, you can't wait for something to begin, or someone has kept you waiting too long, or you're going to be late for work, GOOD! Now there is a refrigerator in front of you. Open it, reach inside and take out a slice of lemon that is sitting on a plate. Take a bite out of it. GOOD! You all have that memory. Okay, I want a TAP DANCE. Look at us and do the best tap dance you know how. Fake it but make it look real. GO! Don't look away. GOOD. Now freeze. Freeze tight like a statue, do not move a muscle! Stay frozen until further notice. Don't even blink."

"When I clap my hands, freeze in one movement into a different position. Make it an interesting position, TAKE RISKS! Okay, ready? (Clap) Freeze tight! (Clap, pause, clap, pause etc..) Now you are very very old, you have a cane in one hand, look at us, your back hurts and you are bent over. Get into it. Now, not all old people are like this, but in theatre this is the easiest way to convey old to your audience. Reach into your back pocket, grab a handkerchief and wipe your spectacles and then put them back on. As you hold your cane your hand shakes. Now, in that character, move off the stage and into your seat . . . slowly, stay in character. OOPS, your foot is sticking to your gum, OHHHH.... OH, WELL, make it to your seat. Stay in character until you sit."

As you can see, this exercise can take on many dimensions and can be a wonderful class tool. It can be simple or complex, long or short. It can be used solely as an ICE BREAKER or specifically as character development for the play you will produce.

It can also be used to teach performers about other aspects of theatre. For example: "You are in the dressing room after the performance. You want your costume to be ready for the next night's performance. You carefully hang it up on the costume rack. You put all your personal belongings into your bag." Etc.

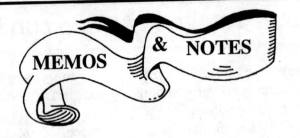

BOWS

Take A Bow 8

You are probably thinking, "What is this exercise doing at the beginning of the book, it should be at the end of the book." Well, in my book it is important to learn to take a bow first thing. It is a great ice breaker. Everyone knows how to bow. Even if they have never taken a bow before themselves, they have seen dozens of other people do it on T.V. and on the stage. The great thing about learning bows first, is that the participants get to experience a little piece of the glory of being onstage immediately. Participants love this game.

This assignment is a very short, nonthreatening game that accomplishes three goals.
1) Teaches the many forms of Bows by the participants watching each other's ideas.
2) Gives each participant a nonthreatening experience of performing in front of an audience.
3) Develops good audience participation for the other students as they clap and cheer for the student taking a bow.

NOTE: One of the most important things for a performer to learn is to be a good audience. It is one of the best ways to learn and it is vital to your classroom or drama workshop!

<u>**ASSIGNMENT:**</u>
   1) ENTRANCE
   2) BOW
   3) EXIT

The assignment here is for each participant to enter to center stage. Each will walk or run or strut; be proud, triumphant, grand, or any appropriate entrance to match the bow. Then execute the bow, with lots of audience response. It is important here that the other students, as the audience, are totally involved: whistling, cheering, clapping, etc. After the bow, the participant then does the appropriate exit.

MEMOS & NOTES

1) This is a short group assignment. The instructions are basically the same as the preceding assignment except it is done in groups of two or three. Break up into groups and disperse into different corners of the room to create a group entrance. Bowing and exiting is done in complete synchronization!

2) It is important to do (#1) before doing (#2) as a natural progression. Same instructions except now we are adding a bit of physical comedy. It is up to each group to develop a small physical relationship before, during or after the actual bow.

EXAMPLE:

BEFORE: They can enter from different sides of the stage.

DURING: Bow in different directions.

AFTER: Bump into each other on the way out. Think of Laurel and Hardy, Clowns, Rag Dolls and Gangsters.

Name Games

Name games are a wonderful way to break the ice in any situation. Everyone knows his or her own name and they are used to saying it regularly. Name games are a nonthreatening way to encourage participation, not to mention getting to know each other's names. They are also good exercises in memory. Memory is one of the key elements to acting. Memory is like a muscle, it gets bigger and stronger with use. These games can be used several times at the beginning of an ongoing class or in a performance situation.

Playing Favorites   10

Ask the group to form a circle. Then going around the circle, starting with you, the coach, each person will say his or her name and his or her favorite color, or favorite animal, or . . . Encourage them to speak up right from the beginning so that the entire group can hear every word they say. Go around once. The next time, the second person will say the first person's name and their favorite color, then their own name and their favorite color. The third person will say the first two names and favorites and then their own. It continues around until the last person has a lot to remember.

Names With Movement   11

Form a circle. Each participant will walk to the center of the circle, stop and say his or her name and perform a movement to accent the name. The movement should be one big, descriptive movement with a freeze at the end. The rest of the group, remaining in a circle, will then imitate the exact movement and vocal quality as they say that person's name. Take turns going around the circle. This accomplishes two things: 1) Movement helps activate the memory; and 2) The participants will begin immediately to learn to put movement to words.

PASSING THE PULSE

Passing the pulse is a tradition in theatre companies everywhere. Following is a simple outline of how to pass the pulse so that your group may also participate in the tradition. Included are some new and innovative ways to pass the pulse. Passing the pulse is generally used as a warm up in classroom situations and in pre-performance warm-ups. It is a wonderful way to get everyone centered and see where the concentration levels are.

Passing The Pulse | 12

Gather the group into a circle and hold hands. You, as the coach, will explain that when they feel their hands being squeezed they need to respond by squeezing the hand next to them, opposite the receiving hand. You will pass the first pulse either to your right or to your left. Now, as the coach, encourage them to anticipate the pulse and pass it as quickly as possible. You want it to move around the circle like electricity through a wire. You will find that even when the group is experienced with the pulse, there will be slow days and fast days, and what you want to encourage is consistency. Consistency is the whole crux of many an actor's/actress' success; or in any field for that matter. So get the group to be comfortable with just standing there passing the pulse and nothing else. Ask for complete silence; no laughing or giggling, no comments, even encourage them to not think for these few moments. For most people it takes real training to learn not to think and just let things happen. Nonthinking creates space for vulnerability, and vulnerability is everything onstage. Nonthinking helps in training cast members to be quiet backstage. Now have fun with it. Pass it to the right, then pass it to the left. Start two or three pulses in the same direction, always reminding the group to keep totally silent as in mime. Let different participants begin the pulse. Create a nonthinking atmosphere.

Passing The Pulse With Movement | 13

Now pass the pulse, but do a movement with it so that the eye can follow the pulse around the circle. Start with a head turn. If the pulse is going to the right, turn the head to the right on the moment you receive the pulse. Watch it go like lightning! Keep it going. Then do other moves, make them up. Jump into the middle of the circle, crouch, all follow the leader. Then ask each participant to create his or her own move as the pulse passes.

Passing The Pulse With Words and Sounds | 14

Next, without disrupting the sacred quiet space of nonthinking that you have now developed, add short words and sounds. Use the word "Yes" then the word "No". Allow no more time than it takes to pass the pulse. This is good practice saying short words with power. Other words are: O.K., Ouy, Maybe, Soon, etc.

Now, try sounds; use the vowels. Circle once with A, then E, and so on. Vowels need a lot of work, although, not as much as consonants!

Some of the hardest sentences to say in theatre are sentences of one word like 'Yes', 'No' or 'Maybe'. It is important not to throw away a word, not even one. There are many stories of actors who have 'stolen' a scene with only a word or a sentence or even with totally silent roles. Here applies, "THERE ARE NO SMALL PARTS, ONLY SMALL ACTORS". On the other hand many actors and actresses can deliver a multitude of lines, but when it comes to a single syllable they tend to throw it away, not giving that word the attention it deserves. Another difficulty is a word repeated; the point here being to vary it each time it is spoken. I knew an actress once who, playing the heroine in a melodrama, had to say the word 'NO' about twenty times in a row to the villain. At first, she had a hard time until she went inside herself and just let it flow out anyway it would, which gave each 'NO' she uttered a life of it's own. Each one became varied and interesting. It gave the scene an interesting twist.

BEFORE BEGINNING THIS EXERCISE ASK THE FOLLOWING QUESTIONS:

1) How many ways are there to say the word 'NO'?
ANSWER: **INFINITY!!!!**

2) How many ways are there to say the word 'YES'?
ANSWER: **INFINITY!!!!**

3) Is the word 'NO' always negative?
ANSWER: **OF COURSE NOT!**

4) Is the word 'YES' always positive?
ANSWER: **NO.**

How many ways are there to say YES?

Infinity !!

Yes, No, Maybe | 15

Ask the participants to think about each word as they say these three words, so that it produces a thought pattern. Go around the circle with each participant saying - thinking, 'YES, NO, MAYBE'.

Yes - No | 16

A) As the coach, pick an emotion and say the word 'NO' passing it around the circle . . . each participant imitating. Do this about three times around with three different emotions. It should pass quickly like electricity. Then do the same with the word 'YES'.

B) Let each participant choose a way to say 'NO' and have the group imitate, one at a time, going around the circle passing it like electricity. The same with the word 'YES'. Imitation is one of the best ways of learning.

C) Then do the circle with each participant saying the word 'NO', each in a different way, remind them that the word 'NO' is used positively as well as negatively. Do the same with the word yes.

No, No, No, No, No - Yes, Yes, Yes, Yes!!! | 17

Let each participant take a turn saying a series of 'NOs' or 'YESES', varying each one, finding as many ways as they can, running them together.

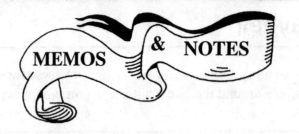

Pass The Emotion

This exercise is another one of my mainstays in teaching. I usually do it before or after the "Freeze-walk." It is an exercise that can be used in a one-time workshop situation or used as a daily warm-up. It can develop into some very interesting in depth work. It is an opportunity for participants to try out saying different lines with various emotions. It is a chance to try their voices, to experiment.

Create a circle. First, pass the emotions without speaking. Examples: boredom- shift your hip and heave a big sigh, or, anger- stamp your foot and let out a throat grunt, or, bashful- cross one leg over the other, fold your hands behind you, look down at your feet, then slowly lift your head part way to see who is looking. This gives the participants the opportunity to get the correct facial expressions and physical movements.

Now add in lines that are improvised on the spot. Start with a line that you, as the coach, make-up, and, going around the circle, have each participant repeat it in his or her own way. Go through the various emotions creating a new line for each one.

As soon as the participants get the idea, they will create their own lines. State the emotion and let them come up with a line that fits that emotion. This develops improvisational skills. Then let everyone choose their own emotion as the group circles around.

As you can see, this exercise can develop in many directions. It gives everyone the opportunity to perform in front of the group under nonthreatening conditions. It is a game that participants don't seem to ever tire of.

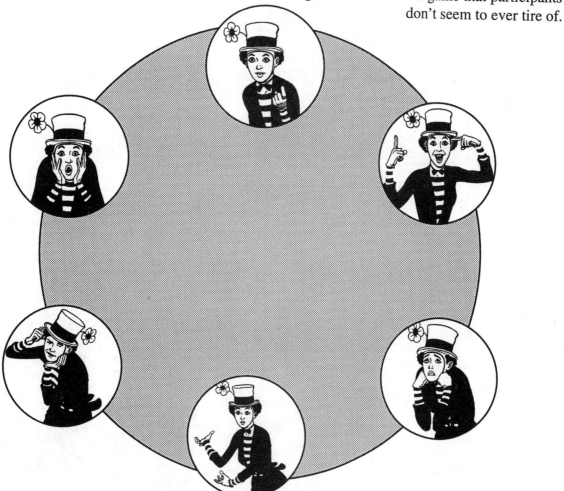

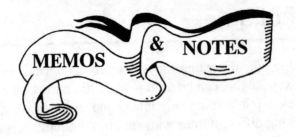

MEMOS & NOTES

WEATHER GAME - CIRCLE

Pick A Weather | 19

A very effective technique to help an actor establish his or her whereabouts, which can be important in developing a character, is to decide upon the weather. This exercise is designed to practice in a variety of weather conditions. Please keep in mind that this is mime and that no sound should be made.

The group is in a wide circle. You may begin by picking a weather condition yourself but do not tell anyone. Go to the center of the stage and experience it. Let the group guess what it is. Let each participant take a turn. EXAMPLE WEATHER CONDITIONS: Snow, Heat, Rain, Cold, Wind, Sleet, Hurricane, Etc . . .

ASSIGNMENT:
1) **Decide on a weather condition.**
2) **Go to the center of the circle.**
3) **Experience the weather condition.**
4) **Freeze when you are finished.** (As the coach you may need to ask them to freeze.)

Weather Walk | 20

Have each participant walk from one side of the stage to the other in a chosen weather condition. Each time the weather condition is assigned by the coach, a classmate, or picked out of a hat.

ICE SCULPTURES

This is a very popular set of games. Each game goes very quickly so you can play it many times or play it a few times for a warm-up.

Strike A Pose | 21

This exercise is simple and effective for developing many skills. It teaches the participants to listen and respond spontaneously. It enhances the use of simple, sharp movements and gives everyone a lesson in spatial awareness. One of the most important things for any actor/actress to remember is that when they are on stage, they own the space and it is there to be used. For instance, a single movement that coincides with the most important word in a spoken sentence can enhance the meaning tenfold. For instance, an arm raised in a right angle above the head increases the acting space to include the angle of the arm.

The group should spread out in the room or be up on the stage. When you, as the coach, clap your hands everyone should strike a pose and freeze tight without a twitch. It doesn't matter what the first pose is. From then on when you clap your hands each participant will strike a new pose. You will do a series of claps and they will pose each time in a new position. Remind them to take risks and make each and every pose interesting like a work of art. Vary your claps; at first, be slow and consistent giving participants time to find their poses. Then at different intervals, increase or vary the speed. End with claps in rapid succession so that the switching of poses resembles dancing.

FOLLOW-UP EXERCISE: Now ask them to strike the pose placing their bodies high, on their toes, reaching up and freezing. Now ask them to find a pose in the middle level and freeze. Next, ask them to strike a pose in the low range, which should bring them down to the floor. Freeze. Now each time you clap, they will strike a pose, each time at a different level. Remind them to take risks!

No one should use the same level twice. If the first pose is high; then the next one must be medium or low. If the second pose is low; then the third pose must be high or medium and so on. As in any of these exercises, you may want to let the participants take turns being the coach by providing the claps.

Run, Pose, Freeze | 22

     You need a cleared space, either a stage, or a room with furniture pushed aside. Ask the class to line up single file at one corner. Pick a leader, a different leader each time. The leader will run in a diagonal line to the opposite corner of the room or the stage. When he or she reaches the corner this leader will strike an interesting pose and freeze, choosing either High, Medium or Low, and will remain completely frozen throughout the exercise. The next participant then runs to join the first by touching one body part but at a different level. So, if the first player chooses High, the next player must pick Medium or Low and if the second player picks Low, the third player must pick Medium or High and so on. **Each player must touch the next player but no two players may touch adjacent players at the same level.**

NOTE: Each consecutive player does not have to touch the player who ran before, but instead, can touch any player and should be encouraged to do so to produce more interesting Ice Sculptures. As the coach, keep reminding them to stay frozen until you give the command to do otherwise. Also, remind them to take RISKS, to make each move as interesting as possible.

Run, Pose, Freeze With Emotions | 23

     Same exercise as before but this time as each player strikes a pose he or she will also put on a facial emotion that you as the coach will name. For instance, the coach will say "anger", and as each player lands he or she will put on an angry face. Ask them to exaggerate their faces to make the sculpture more dynamic. You will be amazed at the "art piece" that they will create. In fact, if a teacher brings in a polaroid camera to take a picture of each Ice Sculpture that is made, the players will get such a big kick out of seeing a picture of what they have just created they will strive even harder on the next one!

SOME SUGGESTED EMOTIONS: Disgusted, Angry, Happy, Sad, Emotionally Disturbed, etc. Remember the Ice Sculptures are more effective with big emotions.

MEMOS & NOTES

WARM-UP EXERCISES FOR PERFORMING CASTS

Another use of working on 'how' we say things rather than relying on 'what' we say, is to take lines that are already learned for a play and work with them. Everyone has an idea of how a line can be said and it is very revealing to learn from peers. The valuable ingredient here is spontaneity. Sometimes our first instincts are the best. It is vital for an actor to get in touch with his or her instincts, to use them and to trust those instincts. But often the entire process of becoming an actor is to tear down the programmed barriers and to become completely vulnerable. Then and only then can we find the truth in each sentence uttered. This is why most children are such natural actors and actresses. They haven't built up the layers of social patterns that most adults have to work through. On the other hand someone who has lived a full life can be more believable in every word uttered. It is a matter of tapping into life experiences, which many adults do quite naturally. A natural actor, whether adult or child is someone who uses instincts and who is not afraid to break through all barriers.

Acting is 'not' *acting.* So many times a person new to the stage, especially adults, will put on a totally unnatural voice every time they get in front of people, not realizing that their most valuable asset is being themselves with voice projection. I'll never forget a time, years ago, when I auditioned for a group of directors. I finished my monologue, and one of the directors, a very prominent man in his field, said something that changed my approach to acting forever. He said, "You have one of the most wonderful voices I have ever heard, when you introduced yourself. But when you started your monologue your voice changed to an almost unusable quality. Use your real voice."

These exercises accomplish many things. One, they let the actor hear a variety of ways to say his or her line. Two, they let each actor in turn have a chance to say many lines spontaneously, allowing for plenty of experience in using instincts. It also gives you as director/coach an opportunity to sharpen and hone various lines. Remind the actors of their diction and projection. These exercises can be used all the way through the play process. They can be used to help learn troubling lines. They can be check points throughout, and are wonderful warm-ups before a show.

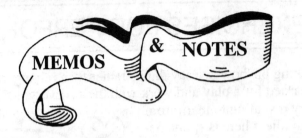

I Say Your Line - You Say My Line | 24

Gather the group into a circle and ask everyone to close their eyes and think of an entire sentence that they speak in the play or musical. It should be a sentence of five words or more, however, avoid paragraphs. If a cast member doesn't have any lines, they should choose a line from the play.

One by one, each cast member says his or her line the way they are said in the play; then, going around the circle, the rest of the cast says that very same line individually giving that particular cast member different ideas on how to say that particular line. As the play progresses, you as the director, may want to select certain lines that need work; or perhaps the actor simply needs to hear others say his or her line with the proper emphasis to get it clearly in mind.

Echoes | 25

Another warm-up that is effective for stimulating the brain and voice is to have each cast member in the circle silently think of a sentence that he or she says in the performance. Then go around the circle with one cast member at a time saying this sentence to the opposite wall followed by the rest of the cast saying it back in unison. This will lock brains into gear and give voices an excellent warming.

One - Two - Three ! | 26

This can be done several times in succession, using a different sentence each time. Ask the cast members to think of a sentence, and then on the count of three, everyone will say this sentence at the same time. Remind them to project, not yell. Then ask them to vary the same sentence; whispering it, screaming it, using various emotions.

ENUNCIATING

Enunciation is perhaps the most essential ingredient of any kind of speaking whether it is on stage, giving a lecture or in our everyday lives. Sometimes enunciation can make all the difference in how effectively we communicate.

For the past seven years our theatre company has been working in an old historical building that used to be a very large foundry, machine shop and blacksmith shop. It is built out of stone, wood and cement. Although it is full of charm and ambiance, it is not a real theatre and as you can imagine it has some tremendous problems. One of these problems is the sound. It is possibly the worst room I have ever been in for sound and projection. It absolutely eats every word that is spoken. Therefore we have had to train everyone, even seasoned actors, how to be to be heard in that room. Anyone working in that theatre would have no problem being heard and understood in any regular theatre.

Enunciation is everything. Everything! It can be used 75% more effectively than projection. Projection is important, but projection without enunciation only produces noise. An example of this which I often use in my lectures, is our musical director. She has an extremely soft voice. It is often hard to hear her in class and other noisy situations. Well, a few years ago, she played the Queen of Hearts in "Alices in Wonderland." She was the only actor/actress that spoke so I could understand every word she said. Because of her musical training, she enunciates perfectly. She hardly raised her voice but her vowels and consonants carried her voice to every corner of the room.

Vowels are important, but without consonants to close them off you are only producing native noises. Most people, especially in America, are lazy speakers. Most people speak in vowels and that is why we have such a problem with diction. There is a young woman with cerebral palsy who works with our theatre company. She comes from a community-based organization called, "The Neighborhood Center for the Arts." This organization takes on people with various disabilities and gives them work and trains them to function within the community. This particular young woman is a very organized worker, works backstage, and from time to time, performs in a production. When she came to work with us she was an excellent example of a lazy speaker. One day I was watching her mouth as she spoke. She is a very excitable young lady and I noticed that her mouth was constantly smiling as she spoke. Her mouth never moved, all I could hear was a slur of vowels. Although I understood her better than when she had first arrived, I still had a difficult time understanding what she was saying. I usually had to ask her to repeat herself which was frustrating for both of us.

It suddenly dawned on me that she never used consonants. I got very excited and told her that I didn't think she had a speaking problem, but that she was a lazy speaker like so many other Americans. I worked with her a little while on the spot and told her that if she moved her mouth and would enunciate her consonants, I thought she could improve a 100%. She immediately tried this and right away we could understand what she was saying without repeating every sentence. She was willing to work on it and she is continuing to improve everyday. Now, every time I see her, I tell her if she has missed a consonant. Together we are fine tuning her communication skills. I now think that whether a person has a disability or not, we all have attitudes to work through.

Our theatre company has been forced into finding effective techniques to teach our workshop participants and our performers how to speak correctly. But I suggest that any theatre company, or classroom, conduct as vigorous a training just to make sure that all the bases are covered. The following exercises are designed primarily to create good habits in enunciation.

Let's Over Enunciate   27

Gather the group into a circle. Pick a sentence, any sentence from a piece of poetry, a line from a play, from a famous speech, etc. For instance; "All the world's a stage and all the men and women, merely players." Go around the circle as each participant says that same sentence, over enunciating e-ver-y syllable and e-ver-y vowel and es-pe-cia-lly e-ver-y <u>con</u>-<u>so</u>-<u>nant</u>. Every word should be exaggerated and stretched. Their mouths should be working vigorously, big and rounded, opening and shutting. Punctuate the beginning and ending consonants of each word.

This exercise can and should be used often. It can be used in warm-ups before performances. Each actor/actress should use a line from the play or musical.

When many actors/actresses think that they are over enunciating, you will find yourself saying, "That's what I want you to do on stage!"

BREAKING DOWN THE SOUNDS

There are only two kinds of sounds; vowels and consonants. Generally speaking, one cannot exist without the other. The vowels are soft and are usually surrounded by consonants, which are hard and provide the body for our words. We cannot speak merely in vowels, (Which many people unwittingly try to do), and we cannot speak only in consonants. We need both to create language. We need to learn to use both equally to produce effective communication both on the stage and in our everyday lives.

Faces With Vowels   28

This is a circle warm-up for either class or performance and is most effective when used as a habit builder. Review the long vowels; A - E - I - O - U. Now, in unison say each vowel and make a face. Encourage the group to exaggerate faces by stretching and distorting facial muscles and facial features. Our mouths form completely different shapes with every vowel, so our faces should contort in different directions with each sound. The more this exercise is done, the more flexible our faces will become, and the more dramatic mugs we will be able to produce.

Now try it with the short vowels.

Faces With Consonants   29

This is the same idea but only with consonants. Consonants are faster, and click off our tongues and lips with precision. You can hold out a vowel as long as you want, but not a consonant. When they say watch your P's and Q's, they mean it!. Watch your T's, B's, K's and J's too. No more speaking in vowels. Let's hear those consonants. Let's use every letter of the alphabet! It's equal rights for all letters! After all there are only twenty six of them!

Since the sounds of most consonants are unavoidably shorter than vowels, the facial expressions will be shorter, which is good training for real sentences. You, as the coach, may want to go slowly at first and then speed up the pauses in between each sound and facial expression. It is very useful to learn to be expressive in rapid fire.

A vital part in the acting process is to learn to use our facial muscles with versatility and flexibility. Making a facial expression is often called making a "Mug". Mugs can be essential in getting across an idea, in helping the audience hear every word you say. Mugs are especially important in comedy, but it is important that each and every performer learn to use and control facial expressions.

So many times we might think that we are making a certain kind of an expression and, without knowing it, we are doing entirely the opposite. Often young girls or women try to put on what they think is a sexy expression for a certain dance or song by pursing their lips together or raising their eyebrows, when simply by smiling and showing lots of teeth they would achieve the look they want. We often look silly or foolish or send the wrong messages through our facial expressions.

Most theatre workshop spaces and classrooms do not come equipped with a row of mirrors, so this exercise will need to be given as a homework assignment. The time for accidental facial expressions is over. What we need is scientific data. What we need is a research project! We need a mirror and a willing research subject. This is to inform you that you have been selected.

ASSIGNMENT:
1) **Go home tonight and look in a mirror.**
2) **Go through the vowels, just like you did in class, but now watch your facial expressions.**
3) **Get comfortable with your own face. Don't hold back.**
4) **Now, go through the consonants.**
5) **Let your face go, see how far you can stretch every one of your facial features.**

Everyone should try this exercise at least once to see exactly what kinds of messages are being expressed facially. Anyone who is pursuing acting either professionally or on a community level will need to make this a part of their full time process.

This is another home assignment. In the mirror, go through each emotion trying to convey that particular emotion by using facial features. Of course, there are many facial expressions for each emotion, depending on the complexity and depth of the moment. This exercise will enable you to control your facial features and allow you to draw from an entire repertoire of facial expressions that you will develop. It eliminates the guess work.

ASSIGNMENT:
1) **Look in the mirror and go through the various emotions. Watch your face carefully.**
2) **Experiment until you find the exact look on your face that expresses that particular emotion.**
3) **Now turn away from the mirror and try to reproduce that same facial expression by feeling.**
4) **When you think you have it, turn back to the mirror and take a look.**
5) **Keep trying until you can achieve that facial expression on command.**
6) **Do this with every emotion and every variance of each emotion possible.**

After everyone has done some work in the mirror at home, do some in depth work with the group. Comment on what kinds of faces they are producing. Are they real? Is it what they think they are portraying? Help them to get in touch with their own facial features, closing the gap between what they are feeling and their outward communication.

Some work spaces may have enough mirrors to work with the entire group or with smaller sections of the group. If so, you can do this exercise in class. Everyone will still need some private time at home in front of the mirror.

Tongue Twisters

Tongue twisters are a wonderful tool to use to unlock our tongues, and they are a lot of fun for everyone. You may want to go to the library to find a variety of tongue twisters or you may choose to let the players use the more common ones that everyone already knows. Following are variations on a theme:

ASSIGNMENT:
1) **Pick a tongue twister. Let the participants choose their own. Tongue twisters may be used by more than one participant.**
2) **Go around the circle letting each person say his or her.**
3) **Go around the circle saying it as fast as it can be said, trying not to make mistakes.**
4) **Say your twister three times as fast as you can trying not to make mistakes.**
5) **Say your twister using an emotion.**

Toy Boat

Use the tongue twister, "Toy Boat." It is one of the most confusing of twisters. Let each person say it really fast, as many times as possible without making a mistake. (It is extremely difficult until you get used to saying it, and even then it is hard.) Try going around the circle, letting each person say it with a different emotion. You will be surprised how much you can get out of these two short words.

Next go around the circle asking each participant to use "Toy boat" in a sentence with an emotion. This can get really funny and surprisingly expressive. For instance: <u>Sadness</u>: "Someone just broke my toy boat." or <u>Anger</u>: "Where is my toy boat?" Some of the best don't make any sense at all like; "I invited my toy boat over for dinner tonight." Some of the sentences will be absurd but the point of this exercise is how it is said, with what emotion.

"Toy boat" is a tongue twister that can elude even the master.

Blue Bugs Have Black Blood

This tongue twister is perhaps one of the most difficult tongue twisters ever written. B's and L's are particularly difficult. Most people will inevitably say, "Blue blugs have black blood."

ASSIGNMENT:
1) **Say it all together a few times.**
2) **Go around the circle saying it.**
3) **Go around the circle saying it once- fast- try for no mistakes.**
4) **Go around the circle and say it three times as fast as you can. Can anyone do it with no mistakes?**
5) **Point and say it with the emotion of disgust as if there is a squashed bug on the side walk.**
6) **Next step, mime squashing the bug and say it.**
7) **Go around the circle and say it, everyone with a different emotion.**

You may want to give the homework assignment for everyone to try and say it three times, fast. See who has mastered it by the next class meeting. "Blue bugs have black blood" may take a while for some people to master. Encourage them to keep working on it.

Examples of Popular Tongue-Twisters

Rubber Baby - Buggy Bumpers   (Say as many times as you can)

Unique New York -   (Say as many times as you can)

Red Leather, Yellow Leather - (Say as many times as you can)

Thin Sticks, Thick Bricks - (Say as many times as you can)

Say, did you say, or did you not say
What I said you said?
For it is said that you said
That you did not say
What I said you said.
Now if you say that you did not say
What I said you said,
Then what do you say you did say instead
Of what I said you said?

You can have----
Fried fresh fish,
Fish fried fresh,
Fresh fried fish,
Fresh fish fried,
Or fish fresh fried.

A peck of pickled peppers Peter Piper picked;
If Peter Piper picked a peck of pickled peppers,
Where's the peck of pickled peppers Peter Piper picked?

She is a thistle sifter, and she has a sieve of sifted
thistles, and a sieve of unsifted thistles, and the sieve of
unsifted thistles she sieves into the sieve of sifted
thistles, because she is a thistle sifter.

Three sick thrushes sang thirty-six thrilling songs.

I thought I thought a thought. But the thought I thought I
thought wasn't the thought I thought I thought. If the
thought I thought I thought had been the thought I
thought, I wouldn't have thought so much.

More Tongue Twisters

The skunk sat on a stump and thunk
the stump stunk.
But the stump thunk the skunk stunk.
A skunk jumped over a stump in a skunk hole.

If a woodchuck could chuck wood,
How much wood would a woodchuck chuck,
If a woodchuck could chuck wood?
He would chuck, as much as he could,
If a woodchuck could chuck wood.

Beautiful babbling brooks
bubble between blossoming banks.

How many cans
Can a canner can
If a canner
Can can cans?
A canner can can
As many cans
As a canner can
If a canner
Can can cans.

Betty Botter bought some butter,
But, she said, the butter's bitter.
If I put it in my batter,
It will make my batter bitter.
But a bit of better butter--
That would make my batter better.
So she bought a bit of butter,
Better than her bitter butter.
And she put it in her batter,
And the batter was not bitter
So 'twas better Betty Botter
Bought a bit of better butter.

Type up a sheet of longer tongue twisters and make copies for your group. Examples of longer ones that are available in your local library: "Betty bought some bitter butter" and "Moses supposes his toeses are roses." Assign one to each participant. More than one participant will use each tongue twister. Give them a time period in which to memorize their tongue twister at home and work on saying it fast. This piece will be used in the variety of exercises following. If you are in a one day workshop situation, you can still do this exercise by having the participants read their tongue twister instead of reciting it. Following is one of the most delightful of tongue twisters.

Moses supposes his toeses are roses
Moses supposes erroneously
For nobody's toeses are posies of roses
As Moses supposes his toeses to be.

SUGGESTED EXERCISES:

1) Go around in the circle letting each participant recite his or her twister.
2) Go around saying it as fast as possible with as few mistakes as possible.
3) Now have each participant perform it in front of the group with enunciation and projection.
4) Perform it in front of the group with an assigned emotion.
5) Perform it as if giving a famous speech, as if they were a great orators using hand gestures.
6) Sing it in false opera, in the grand ol' style with hands clasped dramatically.
7) Come up with your own ideas.

In the beginning of a workshop or class situation, usually there is nothing memorized. Nothing to work from for any in-depth practice. A tongue twister is a quick and easy way to get something right away to work from and it's an excellent polisher for diction. Once memorized, this twister becomes a format for anything. It goes along with the concept presented on page 51, "It's not what you say; but how you say it."

Writing tongue twisters is a wonderful way to learn about words, letters and sound groupings. And of course if you didn't have time to go to the library it is a ready resource. You can either write them yourself or do this exercise which includes the entire group.

Think of any tongue twisters that you already know off the top of your head and pattern your twisters after them. First you need a theme. Perhaps a letter like the letter B in "Betty bought some bitter butter." Or a rhyming syllable like wood, could, or "How much wood, would a woodchuck chuck, if a woodchuck could chuck wood?" Or like the 'oses' in "Moses supposes."

So, for instance, let's take the letter S. **A slim swan swam silently through the slew.** The letter D; **Do Daring Danes drool?** An easy way to start is to ask each person to list several words that start with their letter or sound, then organize them into a sentence.

SUGGESTED ASSIGNMENT:

1) **Pick a theme for your tongue twister, either a letter or a rhyming syllable. The coach may want to assign these themes.**
2) **Write a one sentence twister.**
3) **Go around in a circle, each writer saying his/her twister and the group saying it back in unison.**

Optional: Now send the group back to write a longer one, at least four lines long. Start with a fresh theme or expand the one sentence that they have already written. Another idea, especially as a class project, is to type up or handwrite all the tongue twisters that the participants have created and make a little booklet so that they can see their own writing in print.

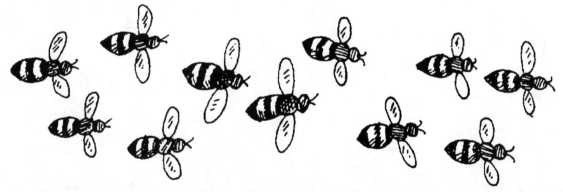

The bouncing Honey Bee Brigade hummed in a harrowing, hostile harmony as they passed billowing bold butterflies and horrific beastly beatles.

MEMOS & NOTES

A SECTION ON MIME

Mime can be an entire art form unto itself. But for our purposes, we are going to use it as a building block. Mime is acting without sound; no speaking, no sighs, no movement noises, absolutely no sound whatsoever. It is a fantastic way to get in touch with your body. Most of the time when we are speaking, we are out of touch with our bodies. We have no idea what they are doing. Mime will break down the components of movement and let us scientifically gain control of our own bodies. The more mime a person does, the better foundation of movement he or she will have to give to acting. I often start a workshop with mime. Beginners feel more comfortable with movement than with speaking. Later I add speech, just like building blocks.

Talk about using memory as a tool. Ask them to remember what it feels like to hold a particular item or how heavy something can really be or how their faces felt when they experienced certain emotions. Memory is a wonderful tool to use in acting. We can all remember how certain things feel, either physically or emotionally. Often it will not be a direct memory, it may be something we saw someone else do, or something we saw in a movie or something someone told us. We do not need to experience everything ourselves to become good actors

Following are a few basic exercises in mime. There are several good books on mime if you are interested in pursuing it further.

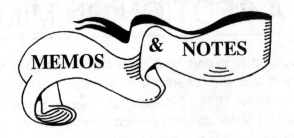

   Divide the group up into pairs. Ask them to choose an occupation that they will do together in mime. For example: Carpenters, Ballerinas, Window Washers, Artists, House Painters, Etc.; something where they are working together at a job. Explain to them about breaking down each movement. If they are holding a hammer and they want to pick up a saw, they will either have to put the hammer down or pick up the saw with the other hand. Things cannot be dropped and cannot be produced from thin air. They must come from a shelf or a box or a cabinet. Send them off to work together in pairs to different corners of the room. You, as the coach, should float from group to group giving ideas and suggestions, making sure that they get a good start. Remind them to break their movements down and to complete every single movement.

SUGGESTED ASSIGNMENT:
1) **Pick a partner.**
2) **Pick an occupation.**
3) **Work out a skit around that occupation.**
4) **Work out the exact movements and facial expressions.**
5) **Practice your piece several times.**
6) **Perform your piece in front the group, either on stage or at one end of the room.**
7) **Receive constructive criticism from the teacher/coach. (Time permitting go off and make it better to perform again.)**
8) **Time permitting, repeat the performance, allowing the coach and participants to note the improvements.**

Solo Mime

Each participant will pick an activity to do in mime. We want an in depth session, finding exactly the right moves that will allow the audience to clearly identify the activity that the performer is miming. The activity should be an ordinary everyday occurrence that everyone can recognize. For example: washing the dishes, cooking, washing the car, writing or typing a letter, calling a friend and having a telephone conversation, planting some seeds, unscrewing a light bulb and putting in a new one, etc.

Stress the importance of completing each and every move. This makes a great on-the-spot exercise, or each a homework assignment. Divide the group up pairs and give them the opportunity to watch one another's performance and constructively critique each other. You may want to assign each participant a specific activity, or you may want to let them choose one for themselves.

SUGGESTED ASSIGNMENT:
1) **Choose an activity.**
2) **Break down that activity, move by move. Try not to leave anything out.**
3) **Practice it several times by yourself.**
4) **Perform it for another person and let them help you make it more real.**
5) **Perform it in front of the group.**
6) **Receive constructive comments and use them to make your piece better for another performance.**

This is a great exercise to do once or many times. It can also be used to help an actor or actress to develop a certain activity that will actually be performed on stage in a play or musical.

Groups In Mime

This is a similar exercise to "Solo Mime" except it is done in groups of three or more. It is an excellent exercise for learning to work together. It is hard enough to learn to work together when everyone can actually see what it is that they are working on, but to work together with imaginary items takes some cooperation. Pick basic activities that everyone is already familiar with. For example: lifting huge stones and passing them down the line to a pile at the end of the line and depositing them on the ground, a team sport, waiting in line, picking fruit, etc.

Remind them to make every move complete.

This can be a very creative and humorous game in mime. It can present all sorts of possibilities. It can be done solo or in pairs. A person will mime the following scenario: enter, and need to use a telephone and locate a telephone booth. Get into the telephone booth and close the door. Proceed to make a telephone call. Take out the right change, insert it and wait for a dial tone and then dial the number. Anything can happen within that small activity. For instance, get the wrong number and don't have any more change. Go through an operator. Have an entire conversation with the person on the other side. The telephone could be broken. Anything can happen! Decide to leave, and the door is jammed! No way to get out.

So now do the basic mime with hands exploring the dimensions, showing the audience the exact shape of the rectangular phone booth. First, the four walls, then the ceiling. Most of us have seen this done at one time or another. You may, as the coach, need to do a demonstration of this technique for your participants to see. Next, find a way out! We need to see the thinking process on the face, and then the expression for an idea of a way to get out. Aha! The actor has found a way out and will show us. Examples: breaking the glass, squeezing out from underneath, going out through the removable ceiling, making a phone call for help, etc.

SUGGESTED ASSIGNMENT:

1) **Enter with the need to make a phone call.**
2) **Locate the phone booth.**
3) **Go into it and shut the door.**
4) **Find the proper change, insert and dial the number.**
5) **Show us what happens. Does the phone call go through or not?**
6) **Try to leave, but the door is jammed.**
7) **Show us the dimensions of the rectangular phone booth with the flat of your palms.**
8) **Think of how you are going to get out. Show us the thinking process and show us when you think of an escape.**
9) **Get out of the phone booth.**

Encourage your participants to be as creative as possible and come up with innovative ways to solve their problems. Each performance should be different.

MEMOS & NOTES

One of the best examples of using mime on stage in a live production is conversation in mime. It is important to teach actors and actresses to never talk or whisper on stage, (Or off stage, for that matter). In many plays and musicals the people in the background or on the side-lines are supposed to be conversing while the main action is taking place. But it is imperative that we never hear their voices, not even a whisper. Any sound at all will detract from the main action. You want it to look like there are real conversations going on, but without the noise. This is an art and anyone can become quite good at it with a little bit of practice.

SUGGESTED ASSIGNMENT:
1) **Divide the group into pairs and designate one person A and the other B.**
2) **Let A be the first to talk in mime while B actively listens.**
3) **Then call B who will talk while A listens. Then alternate back and forth a few times.**
4) **When they have the idea of how it works, let them have a real back and forth conversation with no sound.**
5) **Now, ask the participants to find a new partner to have a silent conversation with.**
6) **Then let it evolve naturally into different size groups with people moving from group to group as if they were at a party.**

You can do anything with this exercise. Let's say for instance that in the play or musical you are producing, there is a village scene. Set up the village scene and let the actors and actresses practice conversing in mime within the identity of their character. Freezing on stage, and well-blocked crowd scenes, with mime conversations, can be two of the most effective stylistic additions to any play or musical.

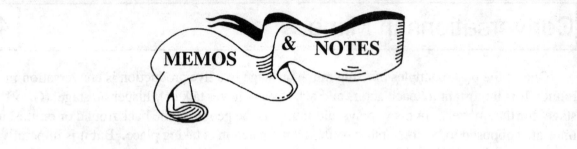

MEMOS & NOTES

Mirrors

Mirrors, has been a favorite among drama teachers and dance teachers, everywhere. It is an excellent vehicle to teach teamwork and concentration. Class members whether children or adults enjoy this exercise.

Divide the class into pairs. In each pair will be an (A), and a (B). The pairs will face one another, palms together but not touching, leaving a two to four inch distance at all times. The coach calls out, "(A)" or "(B)", to be the leader, alternating between the two. The leader will move in slow motion allowing the partner to follow so closely that it will appear that the other person is in a mirror. As you call out, "(A)", or "(B)" it should be un-noticeable who is the leader. This can only be accomplished by complete concentration on the part of both partners. Both participants should have eye contact with each other and should watch each other's movements with their peripheral eyesight. As the pairs get comfortable with each other ask them to take risks and make their movements more interesting. Remind them that this is a mime exercise and that there should be complete silence. No giggling!

The next step is to have no leader as the team learns to work together. This takes total concentration on both parts, and can produce some extraordinary performances.

Do it as a group first then if time allows, sit in a circle and let each pair go to the center and perform a mirror.

KEY WORDS: **Concentration, partnership, trust.**

This is an extraordinary exercise in creativity. It produces true art and will astonish you every time. Get your Polaroid camera ready.

Ask the group to get into twos. Give them two minutes to come up with an interesting pose working together. They must be physically touching. Then call out the word, "freeze!" Each pair should be frozen like Ice Sculptures in interesting positions. Pick out a few of the pairs, two to five pairs, and ask them to stay frozen. The rest of the group will assume the roles of very rich snobs with their noses in the air on a visit to the museum. Furs and jewels mark these individuals discussing the art, many of them exercising their superficiality by pretending to make sense of what they do not understand. All discussions must be done in Mime, showing who they are with movement. When this scene is played out, ask the group to choose new partners and give them two minutes to find their positions, reminding them to take risks and to work together. Choose the most interesting pairs to remain frozen while the other players become the museum patrons. Repeat game as many times as wanted. Try to pick different pairs to remain frozen. Remind them to freeze tight like ICE, like STATUES in front of a bank or in a fountain.

SUGGESTED FOLLOW-UP EXERCISES:

1) You may assign the players who do not stay frozen to become anyone: elderly people off a tour bus, dancers, small children, pregnant mothers, etc . . .

2) This same exercise can easily progress to actual AD LIB SPEAKING. It is a very good setting to experiment in talking to one another spontaneously. Discussing art can take on many dimensions.

This game is a favorite among children of all ages, a game that they ask for over and over again. It is an excellent exercise in mime and in using remembrance skills and imagination skills. It is important in this exercise to remain the coach throughout and guide each participant to the end. It is a great exercise for the individual to learn to take direction. One way to do it is to write down characters on small pieces of folded paper that you will put in a hat. The characters should consist of people you would find on the street in New York City. People who would ride a bus. Examples: Bag Lady, Ballerina, Carpenter, Blind Person, Football Player, Business Man, Handicapped Person, Pregnant Lady, Etc. . . Let each participant come up and choose a piece of paper as their turn comes up. Of course, you may make up the characters as you go along and whisper them into their ears.

The assignment is for each participant to take on all the characteristics of the person they are to be while they are waiting for the bus. They must start from one side of the stage so that they can walk on as that character. The walk is very important. Then they must look along the curb and look to see if the bus is coming. It is not. Now they must do things that their character would do while waiting for a bus. Examples: A businessman would buy a newspaper and read it. An actress would sign autographs. A basketball player would play with his ball, etc . . . It is important here to encourage exact miming, using memory to make each moment realistic. Every so often the participant must look to see if the bus is coming. When each participant has run out of ideas of things to do, tell them that the bus is coming. It is important here for the coach to guide them through each action of getting on the bus. Watch the bus drive up and stop. Wait for the doors to open. Get on. Find money from purse or pocket. Count money into box. And the final action is to leave the bus and return to participants' original seats in the audience staying in character until seated. So, if playing an elderly person, it may take some time to return to the seat in the audience. Don't let them break character. Also, throughout this exercise, keep reminding each participant that this is mime, NO sound!

FOLLOW UP EXERCISE: As the class gets familiar with this exercise you may want to let the participants take turns choosing the characters and doing the coaching.

Do the same exercise but increase the characters to two then three, then four, then try it with everyone playing their own original characters and interrelating with one another, creating an entire scene. For the exercise, when everyone is on stage at the same time, they must line up just like a group of city people would when the bus does come. The coach will need to remind them to keep silent and to relate to one another through mime.

THIS EXERCISE CAN BE A LOT OF FUN, BE CREATIVE !

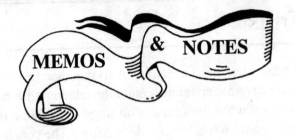

MEMOS & NOTES

This game is designed to train participants in a number of stage techniques that are used in almost every show. The first is active listening, which is one of the single most important things that takes place on stage. Most actors and actresses do not speak through an entire performance, or even a large percentage of a performance; therefore, they probably spend most of their time listening. It is vital to develop listening skills to the same level as speaking skills. Listening can often tell the story just as much as any of the speaking. It is sad to say, but most performers are not taught effective listening skills. The focus is on the 'acting' and when you think about it, the majority of an actor's career will be spent listening on stage.

Another aspect that this game teaches is effective mime conversation, another large part of an actor's career. In many productions there are several people on stage at a time besides the main activity. It is important that in a village scene, for instance, all the characters in the background are active to create an authentic portrayal. You do not want real conversations because no matter what, any murmurings will take away from the desired focus. Mime conversation is a valuable tool.

This game also helps develop effective facial expressions and hand gestures.

PRIMARY EXERCISE: Ask the group to choose partners. One person will be the teller and the other will be the listener. The teller will now tell a story to the listener. The teacher may select the subject of the story, or let the storyteller choose. The storyteller must convey his/her story to the listener, all in mime, actually telling the story with their and with body language. The listener, on the other hand, must listen intelligently, actively, reacting to everything that is being said. After a time ask the partners to switch roles. The listener becomes the storyteller and vice versa.

FOLLOW-UP EXERCISE: Go through the emotions. Ask the storyteller to tell a story conveying anger, sadness, happiness, frustration, etc. . . Or, a popular theme, is to tell a scary story. This gives the listener plenty to react to.

OPTIONS: Of course, as with any partner game there comes a time to switch partners. It can occur often or not at all.

Using stage position language is a wonderful way to communicate about the space that you are using onstage. Even if you do not use stage positions to describe where you want an actor to be, it is a useful tool to teach your students for future performances.

This particular game should always be premised with a small bit of history. Some students will already know this but many will not, so don't hesitate to repeat it to every class and cast. In years past many of the stages were built on an uphill slant so that audiences would be able to see better and to give the stage some dimension. This especially helped in town halls where the seating arrangement was not set on risers due to the multiple uses of the hall. For example; dances, bazaars, etc . . . So upstage is towards the back of the stage and down stage is the part of the stage closest to the audience. The term "backstage" is reserved for behind the scenes, the part of the stage that the audience never sees, where the performers await their entrances.

A chart with the fifteen positions is included on the next page. Please feel free to make a copy of this page and hand the chart to each of your students so that they can memorize the positions.

Start by asking fifteen students to get up on the stage, or in center of the room. Place each one in a position and tell what that position is. If you don't have fifteen students, only fill the spaces you can. Then ask the participants to call out their individual positions. When each of them has done this, tell them to find new positions and without your help call out their new positions by name. Do this several times and then ask for fifteen more participants to go up onstage and take positions as the first group returns to their seats.

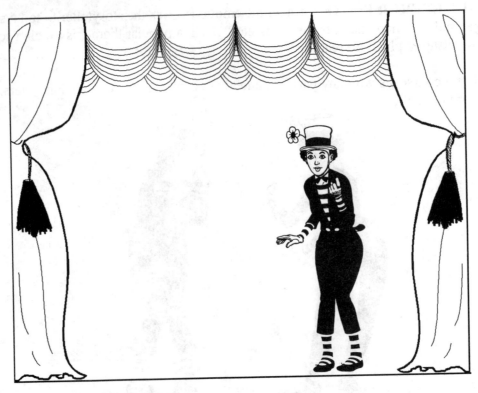

FOLLOW-UP EXERCISE: Let each participant have a turn to go up on stage by his/herself and find each position as the teacher calls it out. Don't call them out in any special order, but randomly.

DIAGRAM OF STAGE POSITIONS

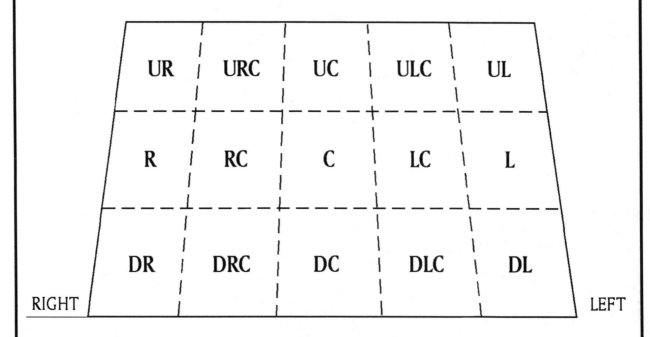

AUDIENCE

Upstage means away from the AUDIENCE, **downstage** means toward the AUDIENCE, and **right** and **left** are used in reference to the actor when he *faces the audience*.

   R means *right*, **L** means *left*, **U** means *up*, **D** means *down*, **C** means *center*, and these abbreviations are used in combination. **UR** for *up right*, **RC** for *right center*, **DLC** for *down left center*, and so on. A designated stage position refers to a general area, rather than to a specific point. This is to be used as a communication between director and performers. An easy way to remember that *upstage* refers to the part of the stage furthest from the audience is to remember that stages used to be built slanting down toward the audience.

I will never forget one summer's evening when I was about twenty. A friend came over to my house and said, "Mila, do you trust me?" I probably said something like, "I guess so, why?" My friend then asked me to go and get my bicycle, which was a ten speed with the handlebars turned upward. My friend blindfolded me and took me on an hour bicycle ride. I remained blindfolded for the entire ride until we ended up back at my front door. I didn't want to do it at first but when it was all over I realized what an adventure I had just been through. I had never given much thought to doing things without my sight. It was an experience that I will never forget.

This exercise is the same idea as what my friend took me through that summer's evening but a lot less threatening. Some of you will have already experienced this exercise in another workshop, but for many it will be a new experience. Besides, it is a new experience every time. It isn't something you can get used to in one session.

Bring scarves or pieces of material that will serve as blindfolds. Bring enough for the entire group to do this exercise at the same time. Divide the group up into pairs. One person will be the guide and the other person will be blindfolded. The blindfolded person will have to place absolute trust in the guide. The guide will need to be aware of everything. The guide will need to watch every step that the other person takes, tell them when there is a step, guide them around things and tell them what is going on. Part of the guide's assignment is to give the blindfolded person some sense experiences while being blindfolded. For example: Smelling food or perfume, swinging on a swing, feeling water, etc.

ASSIGNMENT:

1) **One person blindfolds the other and becomes the guide.**
2) **The blindfolded person needs to trust the guide.**
3) **The guide must take care of the blindfolded participant at all times by holding hands, touching, being the eyes of the blindfolded partner.**
4) **The guide will need to think of experiences within the area for the blindfolded partner to experience.**
5) **After the designated time is up, take the blindfold off.**
6) **Now switch roles. The blindfolded person becomes the guide and the guide is blind folded.**

This exercise is twofold. It gives everyone the experience of being without sight for a short period of time and it provides the experience of caring for someone who is impaired.

VAUDEVILLE - SLAPSTICK COMEDY

Laurel and Hardy, Abbot and Castello, the Marx Brothers and the Three Stooges all became famous for their physical comedy. A physical movement can be the difference between getting a laugh and not getting a laugh and we all like to get laughs. In this section we will explore the world of physical comedy.

Head Schtick | 49

Ask everyone to choose a partner. The assignment is to create four head movements that the pair will perform in unison. Each movement should be separate from the next movement, yet the four movements together will create a whole. **Example:** Both look down, both look up, both look away in opposite directions, and when one of them stamps a foot or snaps fingers as a cue, they both look back at each other with a quick snap of the head. **Another Example:** Both look at each other, both look to one side then to the other, both look away with a snap of the head.

Keep in mind that this is a mime exercise. So let each group perform their head shtick onstage. The main objective of this exercise is to learn to work together with movement and timing.

<u>KEY WORDS;</u>   **Comedy, timing, teamwork**

Body Schticks | 50

Do the same exercise but using the whole body, more movement.

Example: Both back up towards each other until they bump, both turn sharply to face each other. Both throw arms up in the air, then both turn and walk away from each other.
Another Example: Both jump in the air and land in a semi-squat position facing each other, both walk in a circle away from each other and come back to exact spot, both walk forward four steps then turn sharply away from each other and freeze.

Divide the class into pairs. Number One will say, "You got it?" Two will say, "I got it!" One will say, "Well, where is it?" and Two will say, "I don't know, I thought you had it." The pair will decide who they are, Robbers, Cops, Teachers, Kids, Lawyers, Plumbers, etc... They will do physical movements, together, as in the previous exercises, before each sentence. So, four sentences, four movements, head schticks, big body movements, whatever. Each sentence should be punctuated with a joint movement. Let each group perform for the rest of the class.

ASSIGNMENT:

1) **Choose a partner.**
2) **Decide who is One and who is Two.**
3) **Workout a movement that both participants will do in unison for each line.**
4) **Practice the piece several times.**
5) **Perform in front of the group and receive constructive criticism.**
6) **Time permitting, go practice again, making it better, using the constructive criticisms for another performance.**

You will be pleasantly surprised at the performances that this exercise will produce. This is a very effective exercise because it combines the physical movements with the speaking, thus producing experience, in physical comedy.

One of most rewarding responses a performer can get is laughter. Laughter makes the performer feel good and it makes the audience feel good. It is contagious. But to get this laughter you need to know how to get the humor across to your audience whether it is dry or hilarious.

As we learned in the last exercise, movement is one of the most effective means of punctuating a line. Movement doubles the impact of the delivery, because not only are we hearing it, we are getting a visual effect.

Most comedies are jammed packed full of jokes, whether they are subtle or overt. To get a laugh on every punch line means you're going to need a lot of work on your delivery. By using pauses and movement, you can improve your timing, which is everything when it comes to delivery.

This exercise focuses on joke delivery. You will need to find a good joke book. The jokes need to be two sentence jokes, the first sentence being the set up and the second being the punch line. Usually the first is a question and the second an answer. For instance; Question: "What did they call Betsy Ross when they didn't know her name?" Answer: "Mrs. Sew and Sew." Assign two jokes to every pair of partners so each can have a turn being the straight man and each can deliver the punch line.

ASSIGNMENT:
1) Pick two jokes that have two sentences each.
2) Work out a physical bit to go with the setup line and the punch line for punctuation.
3) Practice and work out the comedic timing.
4) Perform the two jokes on the stage or in front of the class.
5) Take constructive criticism and, time permitting, go and work on it to make it better for another performance.

One of the best books of riddles that I have ever encountered is a book called, "The Star-Spangled Banana; and Other Revolutionary Riddles" compiled by Charles Keller and Richard Baker. Printed by Prentice-Hall, Inc., Englewood Cliffs, New Jersey.

This book is full of fairly intelligent jokes about our country's forefathers. The jokes are good and everyone seems to like them, both children and adults. Following are a few of the riddles that you can find in this book.

Question: Why was the Liberty Bell so discreet?
Answer: Because it never spoke until it was tolled.

Question: What was Betsy Ross's reply when she was asked if the flag was ready?
Answer: Give me a minute man.

Question: Why were the Indians the first ones in this country?
Answer: Because they had reservations.

Question: What was the first bus to cross the Atlantic?
Answer: Columbus.

Question: What happened to the Pilgrim when
          an Indian shot at him?
Answer: He had an arrow escape.

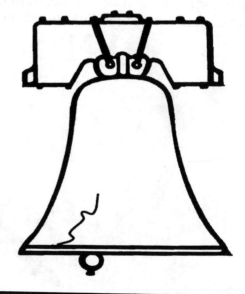

Question: Why is the Liberty Bell like a joke?
Answer: They're both cracked.

DANCE PLAY

Whether you and your class or theatrical company plan to indulge in musicals or not, these dance games are easy for anyone to teach and they develop many things, motor skills, rhythm, music appreciation, creative movement. They also get the participants in touch with their physical bodies.

Most professional mimes have had extensive work in dance to provide them with a solid physical base for their craft. In the world of theatre even if an actor commits himself to being only a dramatic or comedic actor, he will someday run headlong into a musical. It is unavoidable. In actuality, at least one third of the auditions in any community theatre circuit will be for musicals. Some actors and actresses say that they will never do musicals, but once they do one they are usually bitten by the bug. It is important to expose theatre students to everything. These exercises provide some good introductory work in movement which is essential to an Actor, Actress, Singer and Dancer.

Dance Styles | 53

Explain to the group that they are going to use three forms of movement: <u>**flowing**</u>, like a tree in the wind; <u>**slow motion**</u>, like moving through honey; <u>**staccato**</u>, like a robot. Show them an example of each one either by doing it yourself or by asking a volunteer to demonstrate. You may have to help with interpretation. At least in the beginning, it is important as the coach to stay with the participants, guiding them with your words. Dance is often the hardest expression to master, but everyone can dance if properly motivated. Ask the group to move together, trying out each style of dance; flowing, slow motion, staccato, as you call these out. Give them lots of words to help them achieve the proper movement. Single out participants who have it, and have the class watch to get the feeling. Once everyone is feeling more sure of themselves, do a continuous dance; calling out the style, changing often enough to keep it interesting. You may only do this exercise once, or, it is a wonderful exercise to use over a period of time. It is completely optional to use various forms of music to enhance the session. You may want to pick three pieces of music that inspire each of the three styles and record them in the same order over and over. Then mix up the recordings to vary the dance. Finally, when that style of music is heard the participant will learn to recognize it and fall naturally into that dance style. Rotate partners so that everyone can become comfortable with more than one person.

Let's Dance ! | 54

Divide into groups of two. Do the same three dance styles but now relate to one another through the dance. Dance together. Do not mirror each other, (that is another exercise), but enhance one another. As the coach, give the participants plenty of ideas to draw on with the words you use. Then divide the group into larger groups; three, four, or more.

Dance Around The World | 55

Record a tape of various styles of music; African, jazz, modern, calypso, classical, oriental, etc. Use as many styles as you want. Work with your group on each style a little bit. Don't do too much, you want to encourage their natural instincts. There should be an abrupt stop in the music and at least ten seconds in between the selections. During this stop, the entire group should stop immediately and freeze tight until the next piece begins. The change in their dancing should be radical to exhibit the different style of music. This tape can be used only once or if this is an ongoing class or workshop, it can be used often, giving the participants a sense of accomplishment and comfort in knowing what is coming next; a free form choreography, so to speak.

Mirrors In Dance | 56

This is an exercise well loved by all who participate in it. It is important to have inspiring music to spark the imaginations of the people dancing.

Divide the group into partners. Review the mirror exercise from page 37 to refamiliarize the participants with the mirror concept. Then put on a slow piece of music. Pacabel is perfect! Let the pairs move to the music in slow motion but with the idea of dance as the coach keep saying words that will keep them moving. Start with A leading then B, then change to no leader. Remind them to take risks, use levels; up on toes, crouching, down on the floor. Remind them to lift their legs and arms, to bend and stretch, to take chances, and to move slowly while all the time keeping in mind their balance. Their eyes should be focused on each other and they need to use their natural radar. Everyone has radar and all one needs to do is to concentrate. When they are getting comfortable with their partner and some of the couples are actually achieving performance quality dance, ask everyone to move into a circle and sit on the floor. Ask for a volunteer couple who would like to go first, or perhaps you will want to choose a pair that looked particularly good to inspire the others to try harder. The first pair will go to the center and do their mirror dance as long as they remain concentrated or you may want shorter intervals and point to a new couple to take their place without stopping the music. Remind them to trust, and perhaps by this time, you can withhold your comments and let the performance happen.

The art of improvisation has so many places in the world of theatre that it is hard to know where to begin. Of course there are whole theatre companies dedicated to performing only improvisational theatre. They rehearse within a set of guidelines and rules and become very proficient at producing excellent theatre spontaneously. If you didn't know it, you would think they had rehearsed the piece for months. Now, that says a lot for spontaneity.

Polishing the art of improvisation can add to any performance and can, at times of inevitable memory lapses, provide an actor with a tool to save the show and keep things rolling. Often the person you are having a dialogue with forgets a line or rephrases a sentence, forcing you to answer differently from the way the script was written.

Improvisation is excellent training in various aspects of theatre. The most immediate being instant performances. Through the use of improvisational games any group can perform today, right now. Of course it may take a few sessions to achieve a certain level of quality. But you will be surprised at the performances and work that you will see in the first improvisational session. Everyone has a hidden talent for improvisation, some will show it right away and for others it will take some development. It is important to set up the rules and guidelines to make it easier for each participant.

Choose two actors or actresses to take center. At first the teacher may want to come up with the scenarios, assigning roles to each actor. Then as the group gets comfortable, the audience may choose the where and why. Following are the pre-set rules and guidelines to be set by either the teacher or the other participants.

1) **Who are they?**   (Career, job, family, strangers, etc.)
2) **Where are they?**   (School, street, work, office, home, restaurant. etc.)
3) **What are they doing?** (Washing windows, cooking, eating, working, interviews, etc.)

EXAMPLE ONE: One person is a radio announcer and the other is a famous movie star who is being interviewed on the air.

EXAMPLE TWO: One person is a cab driver, low key and apathetic. The other person is a business-man in an extreme hurry, he is very impatient.

EXAMPLE THREE: Two construction workers eating lunch a hundred feet in the air on a metal cross-bar. One of the construction workers has bad eyesight.

EXAMPLE FOUR: One person is a steward/stewardess and the other person is a passenger. The passenger has lost his or her child.

SPECIAL NOTE: At first it may be necessary to give them more to go on, but as the group becomes confident, they will only need to be given who, where and what. Once a person learns to think on his or her feet, anything can happen. It is important to encourage the participants to keep going no matter what happens and to use everything that the other person gives them. It is important not to stop but to continue and try to make something out of the situation. Of course, as the teacher, you may want to censor certain subject matter.

FOLLOW-UP EXERCISE: This exercise can work with more than two people. Try different numbers of participants. Work towards an entire group activity.

EXAMPLE: City street scene; assign everyone a particular character that would be on the street. Give them each a setup and then slowly let them intermingle and develop relationships that would take place on the street. For instance a beggar would get different responses from different types of people.

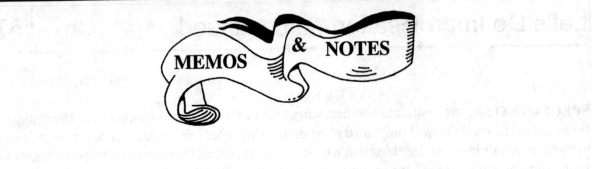

Gibberish! What a word! But it's in the dictionary. The definition reads: **Gibberish-Unintelligible or confused speech or language.** That doesn't sound good. In most cases gibberish would have a bad connotation, but not in the artistic community of theatre. Gibberish is an actual technique used by actresses and actors everywhere.

An actor has to be extremely versatile. But it would be virtually impossible to know every language in the world. And there are those rare times on stage when no one is expected to even recognize what language it's supposed to sound like because it is supposed to be some ancient language from the past.

Let's say your director says, "I would like you to have a two minute conversation in Russian." What do you do? Well, that's where gibberish comes in. For most people, it takes some practice to become fluent in gibberish. You have to root out the basic style of the language you are trying to imitate. Cheat and use some syllables of the real language if you know any. There are some people who can speak gibberish so convincingly that you can't tell they don't know the language.

WARM UP:
1) **Divide the group into pairs.**
2) **Pick a language to imitate, Spanish or French are good ones to start with.**
3) **Let the pairs begin conversing with one another in Spanish Gibberish.**
4) **Go through several languages; German, Japanese, Arabic, etc.**

Tell the group to let it come out any way they can at first. The important thing is to push through feeling silly and begin speaking. The right sounds will come later with more practice.

ASSIGNMENT:
1) **Pick two participants to start.**
2) **The coach or the group will decide who, when, where and what language they are speaking; Stewardess and passenger on an airplane; Father and Child at the Zoo; two Samurai Warriors eating ice cream, etc.**
3) **The two will improvise a scene with the assigned language and the other decided factors.**
4) **Let everyone in the group have a chance to go up in pairs.**

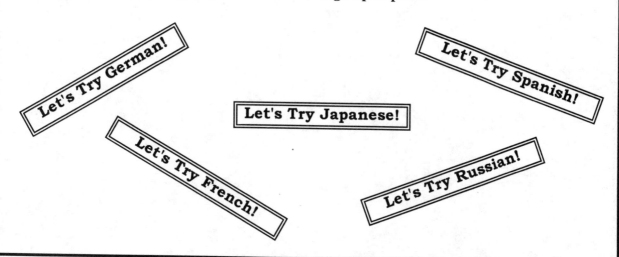

Let's Try German!

Let's Try Spanish!

Let's Try Japanese!

Let's Try French!

Let's Try Russian!

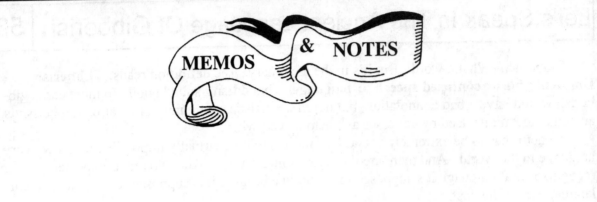

MEMOS & NOTES

One of the most effective games that can be used to teach actors and actresses about the content of what they are saying is this one. Whether you are directing a play, teaching elementary school students, or teaching a public speaking class, this game is extremely valuable. It can help anyone to become a better communicator, which of course we all need to do, no matter what line of work we are in. In most interpersonal situations, communication is the most important ingredient and is often the difference between success and failure.

What this exercise points out is, that it often does not matter what we say so much as how we say it. For instance if you want someone to do something for you, whether an employee or a volunteer, he/she will respond more readily to certain communications as opposed to other ones. If you ask, rather than tell, this person will usually respond by performing your request willingly.

Often in interpreting a script, we take the lines too literally, forgetting to read between the lines for what that particular character is actually saying. For example most people think of the word 'YES' as a positive response. But if that word is used in many different ways, it can help develop the depth of that character. Besides, in real life, we use the word 'YES' with every emotion imaginable.

PRIMARY EXERCISE: You will need a daily newspaper. Gather the group into a circle and choose the driest sentence you can find, yet one that all can relate to, (Preferably about the President or another well known public figure). Make sure it is not too long and not too short, one that everyone can read or memorize. Take the center of the circle and read the sentence yourself with several different emotions. For instance; first as a news broadcaster, laughing hysterically, crying, angry, etc. Then ask each participant to step into the center of the circle, hand him/her the newspaper and an emotion. Pass the paper to each new person who takes center and assign each an emotion. Soon the group will see that it doesn't matter what you say as much as how you say it. This exercise should be done often and can be used as a primary warm-up in a performing cast.

FOLLOW-UP EXERCISE: After letting everyone participate in doing one sentence, choose an entire paragraph and give each participant a copy of the same paragraph but with the assignment of a different emotion. It can be done on the spot, spontaneously, or send everyone off to work on it for ten minutes. At the end of ten minutes, each participant will perform the paragraph with the assigned emotion as a solo piece in front of the group. To take it even further, send the paragraph home with participants to memorize with the assigned emotion, and ask them to be prepared to perform at the next meeting.

Storytelling

Storytelling is a fine art. It is also a wonderful way to bring out the best in an actor or actress because we are all storytellers. Everyone knows a story. Everyone tells stories. Everyone knows *how* to tell stories. Stories are the legacy we pass on to our children, and it is by our stories that we are remembered. Think of your grandparents, and it is their stories that will come to mind.

Tell Us A Story | 60

Everyone is used to telling friends, parents, teachers an incident that has just happened that day or the day before. Ask each participant to think of something that has happened in the past week; something interesting or funny or out of the ordinary. You, as the coach, may have to prompt a few of the participants to get the story out of them, to get them going. This exercise can be done with either everyone standing in a circle or by each participant taking the stage separately. Most of these stories should be of medium to short length.

Finish The Story | 61

Create a circle. You as the coach will start a story. Give it a little thought so that the participants are encouraged to tell it with depth and color when it is their turn. This should be a completely new story each time, unfamiliar to everyone so that an entirely new story will develop. Then mid-sentence at an interesting point, turn to the person next to you to continue on with the story. It is really not important that the story make sense as much as that it is continued on without stopping. The story will be passed around the circle until it reaches the end and the last person will be responsible to give the story an ending. This can be done as a one time exercise. On the other hand, you will find when a group repeats this exercise several times, their storytelling techniques improve each time.

Still in a circle, pick a fairy tale that most everyone knows. "Beauty and the Beast", "Hansel and Gretel" or, everyone knows, "The Wizard of Oz". Everyone knows "The Three Little Pigs". It isn't important which fairy tale it is. What matters is that most everyone knows it and can participate. You, as the coach, begin telling the fairy tale and again, mid-sentence pass it to the next person. Everyone will get the chance to tell a piece of the story and the last person will finish it. If you have a big group and it is a short fairy tale, limit each participant to one or two sentences, it's more interesting that way. Remind the group to project and to be expressive with plenty of description.

Everyone knows a fairy tale or a fable. Ask each participant to think of a favorite classic story. Examples: "The Three Little Pigs", "The Wizard of Oz", "The Tortoise and the Hare", "Alice in Wonderland", "Snow White", "Cinderella", "Rumplestiltskin", "The Little Prince", "Tom Sawyer". It's perfectly all right for more than one person to tell the same story. Every version will be different. Now ask each participant to go up on the stage or to the front of the classroom and tell his or her story. It doesn't matter how much is remembered, or if parts are left out, or if new material is added. What does matter is that they start and they finish and that the rest of the group lets them, without interruption. Most of the remaining group will know these stories too, and will need to be reminded that they will have their turn and to be be a good listening audience. Remind them to give the storyteller the same attention that they will want when it is their turn. One method to insure good listening is to let the more exuberant participants go last.

ASSIGNMENT:
1) **Choose a story.**
2) **Tell the story in front of the group.**
3) **Make sure there is a beginning, middle and ending.**
4) **Take a bow.**

FOLLOW-UP: If time permits, give constructive criticism and let the participants do their story again, making it better, more effective, adding more color and more descriptions.

Put all the stories that have just been told on small pieces of paper and put these into a hat then ask each person to randomly select a story to tell. This is a great exercise to build their ad libbing and memory skills. Give the participants a good talk on making the telling of this story even more colorful and imaginative than the last telling. They should not pick the story out of the hat or basket until right before it is their turn. If someone gets the story he/she have already told, put it back in and pick another. Give them permission to make up anything to keep the story going even if they don't remember or know what is supposed to happen next. The main thing is to keep going and to finish the story. This is good to build ad libbing and memory skills. It also gives a little experience in extemporaneous speaking.

These exercises are marvelous for exposing participants, no matter what the age, to classic stories. Any of these exercises can be done in homework fashion, giving each participant more time to polish his/her performance.

It is one thing to tell a story by yourself. It is another thing to have actors and actresses acting out the story as it is being told. It takes timing and teamwork to work with others and it is exciting to see your story being acted out as you are telling it. The following exercises can be done in succession over a series of classes or you can choose any one and do it separately.

Divide into groups of four or five or more. Talk to them reminding them about the techniques involved in mime. Remind them about telling creative, colorful, descriptive stories. Send the groups off on their own to work on the story that their group chooses to do. Or you as the coach may want to assign the stories or use the hat. The group will decide on who will tell the story. That person will be the narrator. Others will then play the parts in mime. They will play as many parts as needed. You, as the coach, will need to go around to each group and make sure they get a good start. You may have to give them ideas and pointers. Remind them to make their movements big and focused. Give them about twenty minutes to prepare. Halfway through the twenty minutes tell them to start practicing their pieces all the way through.

Gather everyone into an audience and ask for a volunteer group to go first. You may want to choose a group that really has it together to be an example to the others. At the end of each performance, give constructive criticism. Perhaps you can let the audience give some constructive criticism. Then, time permitting, let the groups go off once more to make their presentations better, using the criticisms that they received. It is imperative to stress the importance of energy and exuberance, this is the place to exaggerate each character played. This is the time to be bigger than life. Stress enunciation and projection. If you plan to pursue this into the next exercise ask them to retain the same story that they have just performed.

If you want to, you can let the participants take turns being the storyteller for the entire story, depending on how many times the piece is performed.

Popular Stories That Everyone Knows

The Three Little Pigs	**Sleeping Beauty**
The Wizard of Oz	**Snow White and the Seven Dwarfs**
Goldilocks and The Three Bears	**Rapunzel**
Little Red Riding Hood	**Beauty and the Beast**
The Emperor's New Clothes	**Jack and the Beanstalk**
Cinderella	**Rumpelstiltskin**

Another exercise and a good follow-up, keeping the same groupings with the same stories, is to have the participants of each storytelling group take turns telling the story. Everyone will take turns acting the story out and take turns telling different parts of it. It's sort of a revolving act where one person is telling the story and then steps into play a part themselves, while another person takes over the storytelling. It can be done in bits and pieces or by a paragraph at a time or . . . If done with energy and exuberance without missing a beat, it can turn into a dynamic performance piece. This is a style in which, there are currently various groups of either children or adults performing fairy tale theatre across the country. Some groups tour their local schools performing a grouping of the shorter fairy tales or one or two of the longer ones. Storytelling theatre is a wonderful art form and a wonderful way to learn and sharpen theatre skills.

A SUGGESTION: If you are a teacher of an elementary, middle-school, or high-school classroom, you might want to think about taking all or a few of the best performing groups that develop in your classroom on a mini performance tour to other classrooms in your school. There is nothing like performing for a live audience, and it is a real treat for teachers and students in other classrooms.

This exercise is designed specifically for the director and his/her cast, once a production has been selected. It should be done early in the rehearsal schedule. Many times it is not until the end of a rehearsal period that everyone thoroughly understands the story and the plot. Of course, we would all imagine that if someone is going to be in a production they would read the script several times and do all the homework. And, most directors make the assignment of reading the play at the first rehearsal. But as human nature dictates, many people are procrastinators and the reading never gets done. This is especially true with the performers playing the chorus in a musical. Also, if your cast members are children, some of them can't read yet or read well enough to follow a script. In this case, ask the parents to read the script to them at home. It is important to encourage all cast member to read the script or have it read to them. It is imperative that every cast member knows the story and understands exactly where it is leading.

Even with reading the script, it is often hard to grasp the entire picture. This exercise is excellent for painting the picture early on, so that everyone can move toward the common goal together. It can work for any play or musical.

Write a short summary of the play or musical in storytelling form. Write it as if you had five minutes to tell someone what the play was about including a little bit about the characters. Write it as a narrative. Example on following page. Divide your group up into smaller groups of four to six people. Give them the narrative and have them go off and prepare a storytelling piece, reading what you have written. They can choose one storyteller or they can all take turns narrating. They will all play all the parts. If it is a musical with a cast of thousands, then six people will play a cast of thousands, stylistically. This can be a lot of fun and you will see a foundation being built that will improve the whole production.

When the pieces are prepared, have each group perform the story. After each performance, give comments and suggestions that will improve their understanding of the play and the characters. Open the discussion to the entire group. These discussions will increase the group's awareness and also give you, as the director, ideas. Time permitting, send them off to work again for a second performance, incorporating elements from the discussions.

If you can find the time in your busy rehearsal schedule to do this exercise, it is guaranteed to save you a lot of time and trouble in the end. I have discovered that building a solid foundation in the beginning has prevented me from having to administer first aid before opening night. I call it preventive medicine!

THE JUNGLE BOOK STORY
(To be used as an introduction to the production)

_____: First of all there was the jungle.

_____: Then there was the law of the jungle.

_____: Then there was a little boy named Mowgli who left home to seek adventure.

_____: He was brave.

_____: He was innocent . . .

_____: And, he was courageous.

ALL: Not!

_____: He wasn't afraid of anything.

ALL: Right.

_____: He should have been afraid of everything.

_____: He sang praises to himself and all the beasts of the jungle heard him.

_____: They didn't hear the part about being brave and courageous.

ALL: They thought he said,

_____: "Here I am, dinner, come and get me!"

ALL: Just as the mighty lion was opening his jaws to take him up on his offer,

_____: Mowgli met Baloo, the Bear

_____: And Bageera, the black panther.

_____: They took him under their wings,

_____: So to speak,

ALL: And taught Mowgli the law of the jungle so that he could survive.

_____: But Baloo and Bageera forgot to tell him about . . . .

ALL: The monkeys.

_____: They forgot to say,

_____: "Never act like you see the monkeys,"

_____: And

_____: "Never, Never listen to them,"

_____: And, most of all,

_____: "Never, ever, never go anywhere with them."

_____: Well, Mowgli did all of these things

_____: And all because Baloo and Bageera forgot.

ALL: The monkeys kidnapped Mowgli

_____: And swung him through the trees to their secret.

ALL: Not,

_____: Hideaway in the ancient ruins of the lost city.

_____: When Kaa, the giant python, found out that Baloo, the Bear

_____: And Bageera, the black panther

_____: Had forgotten to tell little Mowgli about the Bandarlog monkeys,

ALL: Kaa could not believe it! How could anyone forget about the mon keys?

_____: So,

_____: To make a long story short,

_____: Kaa, the giant python

_____: And Baloo, the bear

_____: And Bageera, the black panther

ALl: Went to the Lost City and rescued little Mowgli with the help of . . .

_____: Mang, the bat,

_____: Chil, the kite

ALL: And many other jungle animals.

_____: But of course no thanks go to Tabaqui, the laughing hyena and his band of . . .

ALL: . . .   Dish lickers!

***Special Note: This is an exercise that can be used at the first rehearsal. It gives everyone involved a better idea of where you are headed. This will give everyone a head start and give them a better understanding of the play or musical from day one.

Divide into small groups of five or six and send the groups off to create a story-telling performance out of these two sheets of paper. Let them divide the lines up evenly, filling in the blanks with their names. Give them about twenty minutes or so and have them come back to perform their pieces in front of the rest of the group. Encourage them to use lots of energy and movement!

Write Your Own Story Of The Play Of Your Choice

MINI PLAYS AND MUSICALS

This section on mini plays and musicals is easy and fun to do. It takes a little more time than some of the other exercises but is valuable in giving participants a mini view of what it is like to do a play or musical. It gives everyone the opportunity to perform today, right now without going through the weeks of rehearsal. It gives the actors and actresses a taste of the satisfaction they will receive at the end of a bigger production. It whets their palates, so to speak. It is important for you as the teacher/coach to lay a solid groundwork so their mini play or musical can be as successful as possible. Please keep in mind that the real success is in the completion of the project rather than the quality. This is a stepping stone to the bigger production. It is a training ground. Anything that is accomplished is a major success that will lead to more successes. Of course, when quality is achieved this is the optimum, however, give your participants strokes for completing the project.

Mini Plays 68

Divide the participants into small groups of three or four or more. Give them guidelines. Decide if the plays will be classic stories and fairy tales. Or maybe give everyone the same fairy tale and let each group come up with its own version. Or let the groups come up with their own subject matter. Or pick a subject that is real in every participant's life today. It is suggested that you start with fairy tales or fables since everyone knows the plots of these classic stories and would insure a more successful mini production. Then, if it is a group you work with regularly, or time permits, go into creative subject matter.

SUGGESTED ASSIGNMENT AND GUIDELINES:
1) **Pick a story.**
2) **Everyone should speak at least five lines.**
3) **The play should have a beginning, middle and end.**
4) **Decide the parts, and practice your mini production several times.**
5) **Create an organized bow as part of the planning in each group.**
6) **The other participants as the audience should provide enthusiastic applause and response at the end of each performance.**

Send the groups off to work on their own as you float from group to group making sure they are working together cohesively. Give them plenty of ideas and pointers. Give them as much time as you can, making sure that they are still working effectively toward their goal and leaving enough time for the performances. Don't worry if they have it perfected or not. A lot of things will come together in the actual performing of their piece. Time permitting, give constructive criticism and send them off to work on it again to make it better in the second performance.

COMPLETELY OPTIONAL: For either the mini play or musical, you may want to bring in a box of costume items. For instance, supply a box of various hats. Make part of the assignment that everyone wear a hat to enhance their character. It gives the participants a physical item to work with.

This is a fun exercise. It can really get the creative juices flowing. There is nothing more fun than taking an age old fairy tale classic and infusing it with new energy. What you need to do is take all the ingredients and toss them into the air and let them fall where they may.

Divide the group into smaller groups of four, five or six. Let each group pick a famous fairy tale that everyone is familiar with. The whole idea works because we all know how the story goes. It can only be funny and absurd when everyone knows the original story line. So please stick to the best known stories.

Every group will go to its own corner of the room with pencils and paper to brainstorm. They can start by writing down all the characters and the main ingredients of the story. Each group needs to choose a new theme or idea that can run through the story to make it completely different from the original. Something surprising like Cinderella meets Shakespeare, or Alice in Wonderland is a punk rocker, or do a modern version of any of the fairy tales. One of my friends once wrote a modern fairy tale about Snow White who was a singer in New York and the Seven Dwarfs were her band members. Once you get a theme, the rest will come. Use the same guidelines from the previous exercise.

SUGGESTED ASSIGNMENT AND GUIDELINES:
1) **Pick a story.**
2) **Everyone should speak at least five lines.**
3) **The play should have a beginning, middle and end.**
4) **Decide the parts, and practice your mini production several times.**
5) **Create an organized bow as part of the planning in each group.**
6) **The other participants as the audience should provide enthusiastic applause and response at the end of each performance.**

Go from group to group and make sure that they are on the right track. If need be come up with a theme and scenario for any group having trouble getting started.

MEMOS & NOTES

The mini musical is essentially done with the same guidelines. Your only obstacle may be getting everyone to participate in singing. Be sure, in the beginning, to supply plenty of ideas for songs that everyone knows. Knowing the song is 99% of it. It doesn't really matter what the song is. Hopefully it can be more than "Happy Birthday" or "Row, Row, Row Your Boat." But if those are the only songs that everyone knows, use them! You might even want to spend the time teaching everyone the same song or pick the same song that everyone knows. It is more important that everyone participates than the actual song content.

SUGGESTED ASSIGNMENT:
1) **Pick a song or two that everyone in the group knows.**
2) **Create a story line that can include song, or choose a classic story.**
3) **Every participant in the group should speak at least three lines.**
4) **The story should have a beginning, middle and end.**
5) **The song should have group choreography.**
6) **The song can be used more than once. Example: To start and end the musical.**
7) **Create an organized bow as part of the planning of the group.**
8) **The other participants, as the audience, should provide enthusiastic applause and response at the end of each performance.**

Everyone has a marvelous capacity to come up with creative ideas and story lines once their minds are opened up to it, especially children. They may need a little direction but everyone has a story inside.

Another way to approach this exercise is to have semi-prepared pieces ready to hand them. Give them a story line, a song or two, and a few lines for each character to say and let the creativity be put into the blocking and choreography. Some groups will work much better their first time from a prepared script. Keep it short!

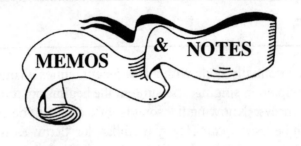

This is a wonderful exercise to help participants become more relaxed and expressive in their singing. It should be emphasized that we are not trying to produce real opera or pretending to sing in real opera voices. Let's use the term "false opera". You will be surprised how expressive even the shyest singer will become when you give him or her permission to sing 'false opera'.

Start by doing a simple circle exercise. Choose a sentence from a song or a poem and sing it in as big a false opera voice as you can, making up the tune as you go. Clasp your hands together in dramatic opera fashion and belt it out. Going around in the circle, each person in the group should take a turn with the same sentence or a different one of their own choosing. Everyone will sing each sentence in a tune made up on the spot.

Creating mini operas is very much the same as the two previous exercises except everything is sung in grand opera fashion. You may use the same groupings with the exact same stories. It will be easier if the participants already know the words. If you have not done the previous exercises then pick a fairy tale or story that everyone knows.

ASSIGNMENT:

1) **Choose a story if you are not using the same ones from the previous exercises.**
2) **Assign parts if you haven't already.**
3) **Remember your beginning, middle and end.**
4) **Block and choreograph every word. Work together.**
5) **Create a group bow.**
6) **The other participants, as the audience, should provide enthusiastic applause and response at the end of each performance.**

Go from group to group as they are working out their presentations and remind them to be bigger than life, to use facial expressions and lots of movement to emphasize what they are saying.

As in previous exercises, time permitting, give constructive criticisms and let the groups go off to make it better for the second performance.

Another idea for music teachers, one that is a little more advanced, is to use this as an opera study exercise. Type up a synopsis of various operas, perhaps using the more simple ones, and let the participants do minis of the greats. The Gilbert and Sullivan Operettas would be ideal for such an exercise.

DIRECTORS AT PLAY

Just as everyone is an actor, everyone is a director. This doesn't mean to go out and find a play to direct. In fact, quite the opposite. Get as much training as possible before taking on such an undertaking. Directing is 98% homework and 2% creativity. Everyone has ideas but the trick is putting it all together successfully. The following exercises are designed to give a glimpse into the creative task of directing so that everyone can appreciate what goes into the process, and be prepared to try a little bit of it. I've always said we would have fewer prima donnas in the theatre world if everyone had to start with training behind the scenes. There would be a lot more respect for every aspect of the process. Until an actor/actress works behind the scenes, he/she can never fully appreciate all the work that goes into a production.

These exercises give the participants a chance to do a little directing and when you set up the ground rules and lay the foundation, it gives everyone a great deal more respect for the position of the director. One of the most valuable things that you can ever teach a future actor or actress is how to be directed. How to gracefully take criticism and how to be polite under any circumstance.

Following is a rough version of the speech I give any cast at the first meeting, whether they are children or adults.

EXAMPLE SPEECH: O.K. For this production I am the director. Next time you may be the director. So let's treat it like a game. Today we are playing in my backyard and we're going to do it my way. Tomorrow we might be playing in your backyard and we will play it your way. There are ten ways of doing everything and we need one person to make the decisions. And this time it's me. Next time it may be you and I will do exactly as you say. I love to be directed. If you have seen me in other plays you will have noticed that I never say a word. I just do what I'm told even if I don't agree. I figure I've committed to that production and I will do it their way. The only thing I ask is that there is one director who will be making the decisions. We need a leader, one leader. I've never seen a production come together very well by committee. We need a person with a vision and for this particular production it is me. Don't give me your ideas during rehearsal. We don't have time. I would love to hear your ideas at the end of rehearsal. And please don't be attached to your ideas, they may not fit into the overall production plan. You are the actor and I am the director. My job is to make you look good. Your job is to do your homework, learn your lines, research your character, give me plenty of ideas to work with. You do your job and I'll do my job.

GROUND RULES:
1) **Once the director is chosen, he or she must finish that particular piece.**
2) **Do exactly as the director says even if you think he or she is wrong.**
3) **Don't talk unless the director asks you to or when you are speaking a line.**
4) **Don't argue with the director.**
5) **Treat the director as you want to be treated when it is your turn.**

This is a quick exercise to use as a directorial warm-up. It gives everyone the opportunity to give and take direction in a short matter of time. It is a little like "Mother May I?"

Have everyone stand in two lines facing each other about eight feet apart. There should be an equal amount of people on either side. If there is an extra person, you, as the coach, should fill in. The first person on one end will call out an order for the person opposite from him to do. That person, without questioning, should do whatever it is then return to his/her position. The order should be short and something that person can do. Examples: Stand on one leg and pat their head, hop like a frog, go to the waste paper basket and pretend to throw something away.

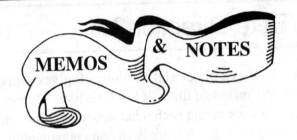

MEMOS & NOTES

This can be done after your group has completed the "Mini Plays and Musicals" section or you may want to include the directing exercises from the beginning.

Each group will need to choose a director or you may want to appoint one for each group. The lines and songs should already be decided on. Read the ground rules on pg. 96, and ask everyone to pay strict attention to them. Send the groups off to work on their own as you rotate and guide them when needed. Give them the time that is needed.

The directors should design the play or musical using their own creative ideas, blocking, choreography, facial expressions, vocal qualities, etc. They will need to give definite directions to the actors and actresses in their mini production. Again, it will work very well to repeat the same fairy tale that the group has been working on, or switch fairy tales around in a rotation so that everyone is familiar with the material but will have the opportunity to do something new. It is suggested to pick outgoing, natural leaders in the first round of directing to inspire the others.

Let each group perform a piece in front of the others and if there is time send them back to work on that piece for a second performance. Time permitting, try to give everyone a chance to direct. This can be done by rotating the stories and keeping the same groupings of participants.

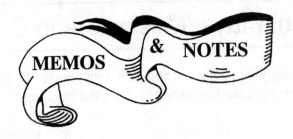

Another exercise in directing is to first have a writing session, where the various groups go off into their own respective corners and write an original mini play. At this time the director is not in charge. This is important. If leadership is needed in the writing, create a head writer position.

WRITING ASSIGNMENT:

1) **Decide on subject matter.**
2) **Decide on Who, Where, Why, and When.**
3) **Give each participant in each group at least five lines.**
4) **You need a beginning, middle and end.**
5) **Everyone writes down the lines as they are created so that everyone has a script.**

Now that the writing is done it is time for the director to take over leadership of the group. Each group will work under the direction of their respective director for the next twenty minutes or so in a rehearsal process.

DIRECTOR'S ASSIGNMENT:

1) **Cast the characters.**
2) **Block the characters.**
3) **Give them ideas for their characters, facial expressions, voice inflections, movements.**
4) **Rehearse the mini play.**
5) **Block an organized bow.**
6) **Give them a pep talk and tell them that they're ready and to ad lib if they forget a line, etc.**

Now the directors are part of the audience. Their job is over until the piece is rehearsed again for a second performance with constructive criticism given by the other directors.

LET'S DO MONOLOGUES

Monologues are a good tool for some in depth work and a chance for each participant to get some personal attention. It is a chance for the actors to grow some wings and try them. Besides developing the obvious actor/actress skills, monologues are a good exercise in standing in front of people. They are a wonderful prelude to giving speeches. There are some schools of thought that preach that everyone should learn public speaking because just about everyone at least once in their lifetime, will have to get up before a group of people and speak. Many people say that giving a speech entails far more personal risk than any other type of performing because it is just you and the podium. At least in acting there is a character to hide behind.

Every male or female who is serious about becoming an actor or actress should have a repertoire of monologues ready and available for auditions. If you are a person who does a lot of community theatre you also need these prepared pieces whether you are an adult or a child. If you are prepared for an audition you have a much better chance of getting a part. Most people fly by the seats of their pants. They learn their monologue a few days or weeks before the audition. Some people can do very well in that short period of time, but most of us cannot. Of course, most auditions do not ask for a monologue, but when it does occur, you want to be ready. The longer you work with a piece the more natural it becomes. It is suggested that every aspiring performer know at least two monologues; one modern and one classical. Of course, if you can increase that number you will have more versatility at your finger- tips. I personally think that every actor and actress should have at least five prepared pieces and ten would be ideal. The great thing about learning monologues is that you increase your brain power and expand your memory. Monologues can be a lot of fun to learn and practice.

Examples of Monologues

Monologues can be short, medium or long. Following are some examples of monologues taken from the play "Summer in Hannibal" which is about the adventures of Tom Sawyer. Included are a variety of different length monologues.

This monologue is given as an introduction to the play by the actor playing an older Mark Twain as he remembers back in time.

MARK TWAIN: (Thinking back savoring the moments) Living on the Mississippi River...them war the days. Life was simpler back then, not much to worry about. You folks probably don't even realize it, but you're missing out on that kind of life, so I thought I'd write it down in this here book, to give you a glimpse of what it was really like. It's like a slice of homemade apple pie, a slice of life, you might say. Most of the adventures recorded in this book really occurred; one or two were experiences of my own, the rest happened to boys who were schoolmates of mine. My intention in this book is to entertain boys and girls everywhere and to remind adults of what they once were themselves, and of how they felt and thought and talked, and of what queer enterprises they sometimes engaged in. See that boy standin' over yonder, starin' out across the river, that's me, that's how I looked as a young boy. I was all boy, which meant I was always into mischief - and just like all the other boys I thought I was bigger than life itself. My youth certainly snuck past me and left me plenty of colorful memories to write about.

This monologue is given by Aunt Polly as she struggles within herself to justify the punishment she will give Tom when she catches him.

POLLY: Hang that boy, can't I ever learn anything? Ain't he played enough tricks on me that I should be lookin' out for him by this time? But old fools is the biggest fools there is. Can't learn an old dog new tricks, as the saying goes. But my goodness me, he never plays them alike and how is a body to know what's comin'? He seems to know just how long he can torment me before I get my dander up, and he knows if he can make me laugh, it's all down again and I can't hit him a lick. I ain't doin' my duty by that boy and that's the Lord's truth, spare the rod and spoil the child, as the Good Book says. I'm a layin' up enough sin and sufferin' for us both, I know. He's full of mischief, but lordy me! He's my own dead sister's boy, poor thing, and I ain't got the heart to lash him. Every time I let off, my conscience does bother me so, and every time I hit him, my old heart breaks. Well, a well, a man that is born of woman is of few days and full of trouble, as the Scripture says, and I reckon it's so. He'll play hookie this afternoon when it gets hot and he wants to go swimming and I'll just be obliged to make him work, tomorrow, to punish him. It's mighty hard to make him work on Saturdays, when all the boys is having a holiday, but he hates work more than he hates anything else, and I've got to do some of my duty by him, or I'll be the ruination of the child.

Monologues.....continued

Little Johnny Baker gets up in class to read his report on the Mississippi River.

JOHNNY: The Mississippi River. The Mississippi River is deep, deep, deep and lots and lots and lots of people drown deader 'en door nails all the times. The fishes don't drown though, cause they're all made of rubber and silver and can float anywheres they wants without sinking a bit. Sometimes on Saturdays the fishes come close to shore and learns the peoples to swim, but it don't do no good anyhows, cause peoples just ain't made of rubber. The End.

Samuel Clemens, who later grew up to be Mark Twain, reads his report on the Mississippi River.

SAM: The Mississippi River is the longest river in the world, four thousand and three hundred miles long. It is also the crookedest river in the world, since in one part of it's journey it uses up one thousand, three hundred miles to cover the same ground that the crow would fly over six hundred and seventy five. A true steamboat pilot cares nothing about anything on earth but the river, and his pride in his occupation surpasses the pride of kings.

Ben Rodgers comes along acting like a steamboat from stage right.

BEN: (Steamboat sound effects until he sees Tom) Stop here, Sir, ting a ling ling! Ship up to back! Ting a ling ling! Set her back on the starboard! Ting a ling ling! Chow! Chow! Ch-chow-wow! Chow! Let her go back on the labboard! Ting a ling ling! Chow-ch-chow-chow! Stop the starboard! Ting a ling ling! Stop the labboard! Come ahead on the starboard! Stop her! Let your outside turn slow! Ting a ling ling! Chow-ow-ow! Get out that head line! Lively now! Come out with your spring line: What are you about there! Take a turn round that stump! Stand by that stage. Now...Let her go! Done with the engines, Sir! Ting a ling ling!

Reverend Walters, the Town Preacher, gives his Sunday Sermon, delivered with power and conviction.

PREACHER: Also I say unto you, who-so-ever shall confess me before men, him shall the Son of Man also confess before the angels of God. (Pause) Well, what's this you say, confess before the angels? I'll wager there's some of you out there who even question the existence of angels. Am I right? Well, God wouldn't have mentioned the angels 273 times in the Bible if they didn't exist. 273 times. Listen up now, God sees that skeptical heart of yours. Turn to Psalms, 34:7. The angels of the Lord encampeth round about them that fear him. You've got the heavenly Father, you've got his son Jesus, you've got the Holy Spirit, and now he's telling you that each and every one of us has an entire host of angels camped all around you and all you got to do is one thing. Repent! Now, brothers and sisters, let's bow our heads in silent prayer.

In an ongoing workshop or class situation give a monologue assignment to each participant. As with any of these exercises, they can be just as effective by reading the material for one day workshops. You can find monologues in your local library either in entire plays or in books of collected monologues. Another great resource is various play catalogues that are in print. They are jammed packed full of books that feature monologues and dialogues. Start with modern monologues and graduate into classical ones later. Start with monologues that your particular students can relate to.

ASSIGNMENT:

1) **Read assigned monologue in front of group.**
2) **Memorize the monologue in designated time frame. Don't stretch it out. Start tonight. It takes the same amount of time whether you learn it now or later.**
3) **When piece is memorized, perform it on stage or in front of the group.**
4) **Take constructive criticism from coach and go home and work on it, make it better.**
5) **Perform it again, and again, and again for friends and family, always working on it making it better.**
6) **Go over it at least once a week so that you can retain it. (Don't lose it after all the work you've put into it.)**

This is a great opportunity for you, as the coach, to give each participant some quality personal attention. Fine tune the natural talent that each person already has, and steer your actors and actresses towards techniques that they need to develop.

If your situation permits, invite friends and family to a small informal performance of the monologues when they are ready. There is nothing like a real audience to bring things together, heightening the theatre experience.

These are also called Italian Run-throughs. Every actor and actress should use this technique to sharpen memory skills and to ensure that he or she has a good grasp on the material. Speed Run-throughs can be used for monologues and dialogues. Speed Run-throughs can be used as a rehearsal technique for entire casts. They are usually done in the last stages of rehearsal, one time. The cast can either sit down in a dark room and run the entire play or musical at double-speed, like a Charlie Chaplin movie, or some people prefer to run it on stage with all the motions, double-time. It can be a lot of fun and very funny.

GUIDELINES:
1) **Run the piece at double speed, don't slow down. Keep the pace.**
2) **Do it with only lines or with movement and lines.**
3) **Don't stop, keep going, no matter what!**

You may end up telling some actors/actresses that they have finally reached the proper speed and to keep it up. It is optional in musicals to also do the songs double time, either speaking the words or singing them acappela.

This is a brain game and actors and actresses are encouraged to use this technique often when rehearsing at home. It imprints the material on the brain and hones in on blocks and weaknesses.

This exercise can be done with any memorized material; tongue twisters, poems, monologues, dialogues, or speeches. Pick a piece that each person does solo and have him or her perform it in front of the group as fast as possible.

Subtext is reading between the lines. What is this person really saying? When they say that they "didn't mean to steal the wallet from the store," are they really saying they, "planned and plotted and actually meant to do it all along," or that they; "just didn't think about money," they just, "knew they needed a wallet." In real life, people talk in opposites. So often we say exactly the opposite of what we mean. Thinking in opposites is a great way to approach subtext. Nothing stands alone. There is always a future and a past. The past is usually the reason for the monologue or the dialogue. So it is up to the actor/actress to come up with what happened in the past to make this character say what he/she is saying. There are usually reasons for everything if only you look. There is a whole psychology in most things we say, and if we can sort out the weeds from the flowers, so to speak, we can get to the real heart of the matter.

In many instances, subtext can give the actors or actresses everything they need. If they can hook into the exact situation and characterization, they are off and running. The more time you spend laying out the groundwork the less time you spend mending and putting on band aids later. This is a writing exercise, but first you should spend some time with the group discussing each character. This discussion will be very valuable for everyone to learn from, and will lead every-one in the right direction.

ASSIGNMENT: (Use a monologue or this can also be done with any dialogue.)
1) **Write a history of this character. Make it up but use the clues that are given to you. It has to hold water.**
2) **Take at least three sentences, dissect them and tell us what that character is really saying.**
3) **Write a sentence with a complete opposite meaning below every sentence. Write them as lines.**
4) **Write the histories between the characters that your character talks to or about.**
5) **Write down things that your character would do.**

If there is time, let everyone read an assignment. You, as the coach, give constructive criti-cism and ideas and have them go back and revise them. Otherwise, give constructive notes on their papers.

Antony: (From Antony's speech in Shakespeare's Julius Caesar)
Actual Line: I come to bury Caesar, not to praise him.
What he is really saying: You bury Caesar, you murdered him, I come to praise him.

Actual Line: The evil that men do lives after them.
What he is really saying: Caesar was good, you, by your deed, have created evil.

Actual Line: For Brutus is an honorable man.
What he is really saying: Brutus is NOT an honorable man.

MEMOS & NOTES

This exercise can be used to accomplish many things. Everyone has a monologue inside of him/her just as everyone has a story. A monologue is a way to communicate that story. Writing monologues can be a lot of fun and a wonderful learning tool.

Monologues can be written about anything. You, as the coach, may want to choose the subject matter or you may opt to leave it up to the participants. Anyone can write about themselves, it is one subject that everyone knows something about. Give the group a theme, or a subject, or some sort of an idea to start with. Or, give them an interesting possibility and ask them to make something up from scratch. Or, give them a character out of a famous book or fairy tale and have them write a monologue from that character's standpoint. For instance; take Cinderella's Fairy Godmother and have someone write a monologue from her perspective. Or take Tom Sawyer and have him write a monologue about the frustrations of being a boy growing up and having to mind his Aunt Polly. Or take Abigail from "The Crucible," and tell us what prompted her to tell the stories she told that sent so many people to their deaths. What were her thoughts? Was she simply trying to save her own life and/or did she enjoy the attention it brought her? Give us a glimpse of what her life was like and why she did what she did.

ASSIGNMENT:

1) **Find a subject character and write a monologue from that character's perspective.**
2) **The monologue should be at least ten lines long.**
3) **Read the monologue in front of the group. Receive constructive criticism and rewrite to make it better.**
4) **Memorize the monologue and work on bringing out your characterization.**
5) **Perform your monologue in front of the group.**

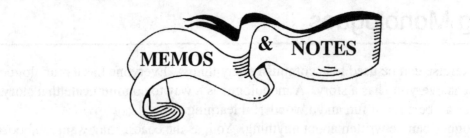

MEMOS & NOTES

This is the exact opposite from what we did in the previous subtext exercise. An excellent exercise in subtext is to have each actor and actress write a monologue from the perspective of a character. This is a chance for the actor/actress to explore and discover where the character is coming from and what the character is really thinking. Look for the clues, read between the lines. Some of the truths will be hidden in the lines of other characters in the play.

This exercise is equally effective for parts with a lot of lines, or parts with only a few, or no lines. Everyone has a past. Everyone has a history. Everyone is important. We all know that, "There are no small parts, only small actors."

ASSIGNMENT:

1) **Write a small history of your character using the clues provided in the lines.**
2) **Keeping in mind your character's motivation from his/her past, write a monologue that reveals something we may not get from just hearing or reading the lines.**
3) **Tell us something we don't know.**
4) **Tell us some of that character's innermost thoughts.**
5) **Read the monologue to the rest of the cast or the class and open it up for discussion, especially if the other characters may be relating to your character.**

There is so much to learn from each other's characters. This is motivation-building and gives everyone a good solid foundation for every word spoken and portrayed. It helps establish how the players relate to one another onstage and offstage.

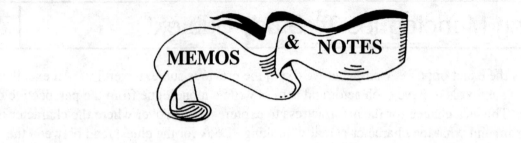

MEMOS & NOTES

This exercise can be most effective in training participants to speak clearly and with projection. It can be a lot of fun to memorize a famous speech and deliver it wearing the shoes of the original speaker. Tell your participants both male and female to think of the typical huffy senator or statesman that we often see in the movies. This image will insure a powerful delivery.

Compile a collection of famous speeches or let each participant do research in the library. A few suggestions are: Abraham Lincoln's, "Gettysburg Address"; Martin Luther King's, "I have a dream."; John F. Kennedy's, "Ask not what your country can do for you, but what you can do for your country."; Winston Churchill's, "Never in the course of history have so many owed so much to so few."; Franklin Roosevelt's, "There is nothing to fear, but fear itself."; Marc Antony's speech, "Friends, Romans, Countrymen,"; from William Shakespeare's "Julius Caesar"; and Richard Nixon's "Checker" speech. Do not worry about specific gender. A great speech is a great speech. As an anonymous poet once wrote, "If it is the truth, what does it matter who speaks it?" It cannot be helped that most of the remembered speeches in history were given by men. There are speeches given by women: Susan B. Anthony, Eleanor Roosevelt, Jessie Haver Butler, etc., but you'll have to look for them.

ASSIGNMENT:
1) **Choose a famous speech.**
2) **Memorize the speech. Know it exceedingly well.**
3) **Practice the speech with dramatic voice inflections and gestures. Do your best to inspire your audience. Drive the point home.**
4) **Give the speech onstage or in front of the class.**
5) **Receive constructive criticism. Work on making the speech better and, time permitting, give it again.**

Sermons make good material for training in delivery. Find a sermon that is in a play or a movie or perhaps there are books on sermons in the library. In my play about Tom Sawyer, called "Summer in Hannibal", I wrote a powerful sermon with the help of a friend. The first production of "Summer in Hannibal" was done with an entire children's cast. The young boy who was cast as the Reverend Walters, had been a good actor up to that point, but had lacked power in his voice. Well, he certainly found his power in doing the sermon. He almost stole the show he was so good. I think it would have been another year before he found his big voice if it hadn't been for that sermon. His rendition of Reverend Walters may have been one of the best performances I have ever seen either by a child or an adult.

MEMOS & NOTES

LET'S DO DIALOGUES

Since dialogues make up the majority of speech in any play, it is imperative to do some work in this area. Besides, working with other people, that's where all the fun is! It is a great feeling to work up a piece with someone else, to perform it and to do it well.

Here are some main points to go over with the group before beginning work on dialogues.

1) **Memorize your material as soon as possible. Know your material.**
2) **Memorize your cue lines as well as your own. (The cue lines are those lines that come before yours.)**
3) **Learn to step on the last word of the line before yours whenever possible.**
4) **Keep the pace going at a fast rate.**
5) **Know your character and the other characters as well.**
6) **Find the motivation for each sentence you say. Why are you saying it?**
7) **Practice active listening skills when you are not speaking.**

Again the library is a wonderful resource for material. Start with two person dialogues. Then if you wish, try dialogues with more characters in them. If you are going to or have been teaching for any length of time, you will want to start a collection of materials. Monologues, Dialogues, Tongue Twisters, Famous Speeches, Plays, Mini-plays, catalogues and so forth. Start a file, even if it is only in a box for now. Finding and collecting resource materials can be invaluable to you.

Dialogues	81

ASSIGNMENT:
1) **Find appropriate dialogue.**
2) **Read through the dialogue several times with your partner.**
3) **Memorize your own lines and your cue lines as soon as possible.**
4) **Practice dialogue with your partner several times without the script.**
5) **Work out physical bits to go with dialogue.**
6) **Listen and react to the other character.**
7) **Perform Dialogue onstage or in front of the class.**
8) **Receive constructive criticism and go and make your piece better; perform it again, time permitting.**

This exercise can be done several times using different dialogues and assigning new partners each time. Whenever possible include the exercise , "WRITING MONOLOGUES TO STUDY SUBTEXT" pg. 111. Only use it to study dialogues.

Example Of A Fast-paced, Witty Dialogue

This dialogue is from an adapted version of The Mikado, one of Gilbert and Sullivan's most famous operettas. Koko, the High Executioner, is asking the advice of Pooh-Bah, a man who wears many hats, and therefore, is fickle in his loyalties. .

KOKO: Pooh-Bah, I would like to consult you on the festivities for my upcoming marriage to the beautiful maiden, Yum-Yum. I would like the celebration to last at least a week and I want to do it handsomely. What amount of money would you suggest I spend on such an affair?

POOH: Certainly, my dear Koko, but in which of my capacities should I advise you? As Attorney General, or as Marshal, Mayor, Governor, or Private Secretary?

KOKO: Shall we say, Private Secretary.

POOH: Speaking as your Private Secretary, I should tell you that as the city will have to pay for it, be as extravagant as possible.

KOKO: Then you are saying, "Do it well."

POOH: Don't stint yourself.

KOKO: Well, well, that is good advice. I'll take it! (Starting to walk away)

POOH: But speaking as the Governor, I am duty bound to pinch pennies whenever possible, we will have to make it an economical wedding.

KOKO: But you just said, "Be extravagant."

POOH: As your Private Secretary.

KOKO: And now you say, "We must pinch pennies"?

POOH: As the Governor.

KOKO: Then come over here where the Governor can't hear us. (They cross left) Now, as the Mayor of this town, what do you suggest?

POOH: Well, Generally speaking, a man is only married once.

KOKO: Then I should do it well and not worry about the expense.

POOH: Exactly. (Koko makes to leave) But ...

KOKO: Now what?

POOH: I have one slight problem, as Marshal, I am duty bound to see that the law is not broken.

KOKO; I see, then come over here where the Marshal can't hear us. (They cross right) Now as my Private Lawyer, what do you say?

POOH: Well, as everyone knows, I am a very good lawyer, the best around . . .

KOKO: The only one around.

This next exercise can be a lot of fun and will really drive home the point that it's not so much what you say as how you say it! Prepare everyone to throw away all preconceived notions and ideas. Tell them anything goes within the guidelines. Anything can happen and will happen. Remind them to take good direction and follow the guidelines that you set up, it's more fun that way.

GUIDELINES:
1) **Know your material!**
2) **Stick to the emotion assigned to you.**
3) **Don't break character and don't stop for any reason.**
4) **Listen and react to the other person.**
5) **Find and use movement.**
6) **Don't hold back just let it happen. Use your instincts!**

You can use the dialogues that your group already knows; or, something that makes this exercise really strike home, is to have everyone learn the same dialogue. If you're using the same dialogue for all the pairs then you can switch partners anytime and have a good solid base for some emotional impromptu.

Pick a pair of partners to begin. Assign them each a different emotion for their part of the dialogue. Tell them to use their instincts and to react to the other character within their assigned emotion. For instance give one person the emotion of being angry and the other of being apologetic. Give one the emotion of being excited and the other sarcastic or apathetic. Give each new pair a new set of emotions to work through and sit back and enjoy the show. The greatest part about this exercise is seeing how many ways there are to say the same thing.

Now, still using the emotions, add in the scenario. Let the other participants help in coming up with who, where, why and when for each set of partners. For instance, maybe one of them is a frustrated stewardess who is at the end of a long flight and is having to help a thoroughly confused and helpless passenger. Now we are stirring the pot even more and things could get really interesting.

Try not to coach during the actual dialogue but keep reminding the participants of the guidelines and throw in key words whenever possible.

FOLLOW-UP EXERCISE: Using the same dialogues give each partner a series of two or three emotions to use throughout a dialogue. The emotions can be interchanged in any order, and used more than once. Or you may want to give the actors an order in which to use the emotions. Another variation is to call out each emotion randomly, allowing the players to change emotions within the delivery of their dialogues.

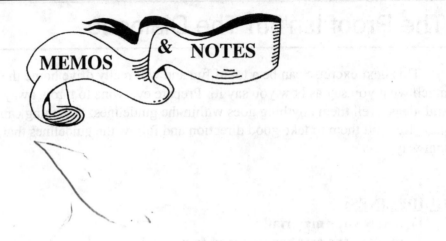

This exercise is very much like writing monologues; except now, since there is more than one person, it is important to decide who, where, why and when before beginning. What follows is an ingredient list. You may want to assign themes or subjects or let the participants choose for themselves.

INGREDIENTS:

1) **Decide who, where, why and when.**
2) **Decide on a theme.**
3) **Decide each character's emotions.**
4) **Determine approximately how long it should be.**
5) **Create a beginning, middle and an ending.**
6) **Write the dialogue.**

It is suggested to break the group up into pairs so they can brainstorm and then perform the piece together. The dialogues need not be lengthy. Give them a minimum of at least ten lines each and see where it goes from there. Some of the dialogues will be good and some won't but what's important here is the process.

Time permitting, you may want to divide the group up into various other counts; three, four, etc.

Example Of Writing A Dialogue From A Well Known Fairy Tale

This is part of a dialogue from one my plays called "Alices In Wonderland." It is a scene that I developed by reading between the lines as one of the Alices meets the caterpillar for the second time. This scene is not in Lewis Carroll's book, it is one created by extending the imagination.

CATERPILLAR: When last we met, you had no idea who you were.
ALICE: I've changed since then.
CATERPILLAR: There's that word again, "change". I find it repulsive. So, you say your name is Alice?
ALICE: Yes.
CATERPILLAR: What does Alice mean?
ALICE: I don't know.
CATERPILLAR: You couldn't possibly know who you are if you keep repeating a word that has absolutely no meaning to you. I rest my case.
ALICE: Well, what is your name?
CATERPILLAR: I don't pretend to have one.
ALICE: Neither do I!
CATERPILLAR: You certainly do!
ALICE: My name really is Alice.
CATERPILLAR: I see.
ALICE: What you're saying is, why be anyone, why have any name. That's the most ridiculous thing I've ever heard.
CATERPILLAR: Of course it is, exactly my point!
ALICE: Oh, you're impossible!!!! (Angry)
CATERPILLAR: Oh, no I'm not. I don't have a name, especially one like that!
ALICE: I'm leaving!
CATERPILLAR; Of course you are. That's a much better name than Alice, if you insist on having one.
ALICE: (She turns suddenly back to the Caterpillar, angry) My mother gave me the name Alice.
CATERPILLAR: Oh, a gift. Well, that's a different story. We must cherish our gifts. (With a big sigh) Some of us are luckier than others (Sadly)
ALICE: (Softening, and walking closer to the Caterpillar) Didn't anyone ever give you a name?
CATERPILLAR: (Sniffling) No, never. (Breaking down in tears)
ALICE: How sad. Here is my handkerchief. (Handing him her handkerchief)
CATERPILLAR: Thank you. (Blowing his nose very loudly) No one ever gave me any name of any sort, except ... just now, when you called me . . . Impossible. (He cries even louder)
ALICE: Oh, please don't cry. It's very unbecoming for a big caterpillar like you to carry on so. I could give you a much better name than that.
CATERPILLAR: You could? (Looking hopeful, and blowing his nose again)
ALICE; Of course I could, but I thought you wanted to be popular with your ...
CATERPILLAR; Popular ... Popular ... I like that name.
ALICE: Oh, but I didn't mean...
CATERPILLAR: Yes, that will do very nicely.
ALICE: But, that's not a real ...
CATERPILLAR: Thank you, thank you, very much. You have given me a great gift. You have given me a name. From now on I shall be called Mr. Popular. Thank you again. (He is now off the mushroom and is leaving)
ALICE: (Heaves a big sigh) You're welcome, I guess.

Writing Fairy Tale Dialogues

This is a fun exercise in fantasy. Choose one fairy tale for the entire class to work from. Think about who the characters are and write dialogues that would occur between different sets of characters; for example, explore the characters in "Snow White and the Seven Dwarfs." There can be conversations between Snow White and the wicked Queen, the Queen and her henchman, Snow White and the henchman, Snow White and Doc, Doc and the Prince, etc.

Now let's avoid the obvious and look for the unthought of conversations. Let's say, for instance, "Sleeping Beauty" is our choice. Now, we all know who the main characters are, in fact, the only characters that appear in the story are the main characters: Beauty, her parents, the good fairies, the bad fairy and the Prince. But think about it, they lived in a palace. It takes hundreds of people to run a palace. It was a kingdom! How many people lived in the kingdom? Who were these people? Rich people, peasants, servants, traveling tourists, entertainers, cooks, farmers, the list goes on and on.

As a group, brainstorm these characters, root them out. Assign each pair of partners two of these characters and let them write a dialogue about the happenings in the kingdom. For instance, two palace chefs can talk about the up-and-coming birthday party, or two entertainers can gossip about the curse, or maybe after the entire palace falls asleep have two farmers outside the briar hedge talk about the mysterious fate of those within.

Another fun thing to do is to write the hidden dialogues between the main characters. Think of instances that would bring two characters together to talk. Try to avoid the obvious ones; for example, Little Red Riding Hood has visited her grandmother often before that fateful day. Write a conversation that she and her grandmother might have had. Or, try the conversation between Cinderella and her father when he told her he was bringing home a stepmother and two stepsisters.

Let each group perform its creation. Time permitting, give critiques and perform it again.

MEMOS & NOTES

LET'S DO INTERVIEWS

These exercises in interviewing can accomplish many things. Almost everyone, at one time or another, has the fantasy of becoming a D.J. on the radio, or a T.V. talk show host, and all of us will someday interview for a job. These exercises are creative and can be a lot of fun while at the same time providing a dynamic channel for training. They can be as simple or as complex as you want.

Radio Interviews | 85

This is a very popular game. In an ongoing workshop or classroom situation it is suggested to start with radio interviews in the beginning of the session. It is an effective way to get the participants speaking in a nonthreatening manner, since on the radio you are heard and not seen.

Set up some sort of screen or block so that the participants will be heard and not seen. You can set up two chairs directly behind your stage curtains or you can hang a piece of material in the front of the room. Remind the participants that they will have to project to be heard through the material.

Divide the group into pairs, one will play the D.J. and the other, the person being interviewed. You may want to assign characters to be interviewed the first time around or let the participants choose for themselves. An easy way to get started is to pick characters from fairy tales, since this is common ground and everyone is familiar with them. For instance, the D.J. could interview Cinderella's Fairy Godmother, Snow White's evil stepmother, the Wizard from OZ, or the Mad Hatter from Wonderland. Or you could pick characters from famous books: Tom, from "Tom Sawyer"; or Black Beard from "Treasure Island"; or Miss Minchin from "The Little Princess"; or Ben Weatherstaff from "The Secret Garden"; or even a character from a text you are currently using in the classroom.

Send the pairs off with pencil and paper to work out a carefully written interview. Designate a minimum of how many questions should be written. Help and encourage your participants to create dynamic and stimulating questions and answers. For instance, if the D.J. is interviewing George Washington he might ask, "President Washington, did you or did you not chop down the cherry tree? Is that a myth or is it reality?" Or if the D.J. is interviewing Snow White's evil stepmother, "Exactly what is your background in evil potions? Did you study with any of the greats?" Ask them to think about radio programs that they have heard and to imitate the D.J. characters. This copycat technique can create quite a bit of humor in the radio interviews.

<u>**ASSIGNMENT:**</u>
1) **Divide the group into pairs.**
2) **Each pair picks a character to interview.**
3) **Each pair needs to make up a station identification and a creative way of presenting it.**
4) **Write the designated number of questions in a dynamic and provocative manner.**
5) **Write a creative and interesting answer to every question that will reveal to us who this character is.**
6) **Practice the piece several times.**
7) **Perform the piece behind the curtain with the group listening.**
8) **Receive constructive criticism and, time permitting, go back and make it better for another performance.**

Time permitting, switch the person playing the D.J. with the person playing the character so that both participants will have the opportunity to play both parts.

MEMOS & NOTES

This exercise is much like the radio interview format. But now we are dealing with a real life situation that sooner or later we will all find ourselves in. You may want to assign the interview situations or let the pairs pick for themselves. The pairs will need to decide what the outcome will be. Will the interviewee be hired, not hired, or will the interviewer say, "We will get back to you later." or, "Don't call us, we'll call you."

ASSIGNMENT:
 1) **Decide who the interviewer is.**
 2) **Decide what position the interviewee is trying to get.**
 3) **Decide what the interviewee's background is. What kind of training and experience does the interviewee have, if any?**
 4) **Decide the outcome.**
 5) **Write a series of questions that the interviewer would ask.**
 6) **Write the answers that that interviewee would reply.**
 7) **There must be a beginning, middle and end.**
 8) **Practice the piece several times.**
 9) **Perform the piece in front of the group.**
 10) **Receive constructive criticism and, time permitting, make it better and perform again.**

Some suggested situations: restaurant owner - waiter/waitress position; principal - teaching position; director - acting position; president of a firm - computer operator position; zoo keeper - monkey trainer position; construction firm owner - carpenter position; comic book editor - cartoonist position; etc.

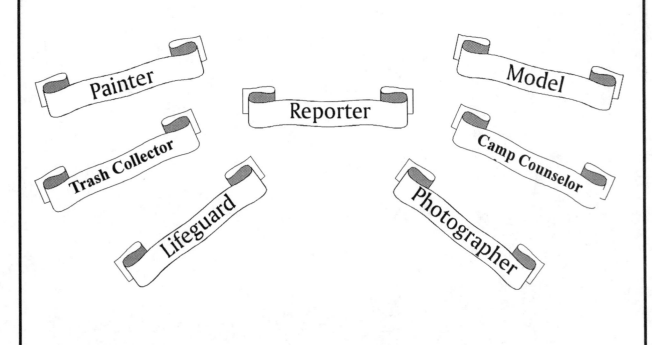

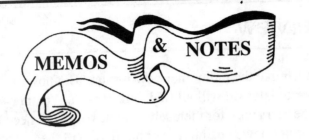

MEMOS & NOTES

T.V. Talk Show Host

This can be a lot of fun. Divide the group into pairs, one being the talk show host and the other, the character being interviewed. Pick one person from the group who is outgoing and versatile and designate that person as the announcer for all the pairs. That person will go around to each pair and write down the name of the "host" and the "character" in each pair and will introduce them accordingly. For instance, if they are imitating Johnny Carson, the announcer will imitate Ed McMahon saying, "Here's Johnny!" You may want to pick known talk show hosts or let the pairs come up with their own personas. If they are creating their own persona then they will need to come up with a name and an introduction that the announcer can use. Even though most talk show hosts are introduced by the unseen voice, let your announcer be visible for the experience. Another option, equipment permitting, is to set up a mike from offstage so that you only hear the announcer.

You may want to pick a series of characters from a category, like fairy tale characters, story book characters, famous people in history. Another idea that can be a lot of fun is to pick actual movie stars and singers of today and yesterday.

Set up two chairs onstage or in front of the class. Send the pairs off to work out their piece and go around giving them ideas and suggestions as needed. When the pieces are ready, do a performance session.

ASSIGNMENT:
1) Pick a talk show host that is on T.V. or create your own persona.
2) Write out an introduction for the announcer to use and work out an entrance for the talk show host.
3) Pick a character to be interviewed.
4) Write out an introduction that you, as the talk show host will use to introduce your guest.
5) Work out an entrance for the guest.
6) Write the designated number of questions. Make them interesting and provocative.
7) Write the answers that the guest would give. Answer with as much detail as possible.
8) Practice the piece several times, in chairs.
9) Perform the piece in front of the group.
10) Receive constructive criticism and, time permitting, go back to make it better for a second performance.

Encourage the rest of the group to be the appropriate audience for each talk show host that appears. An obvious example would be the Arsenio Hall show when the audience circles their arms and they grunt. A nice signature touch would be to add in the line that Arsenio uses during every show when he points to a certain section of the audience and says, "Those are the people who take showers once a month, that's why they're sitting over there by themselves."

Once the pairs have their lines written, encourage them to elaborate spontaneously. Set up the guidelines and let the sparks fly!

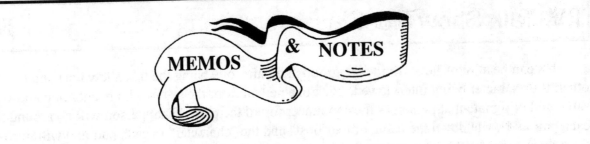

MEMOS & NOTES

Another idea for classroom situations, is to use any of these exercises as a companion to any history lesson. Assign famous people in history to be interviewed, and give the students time to look up facts that can be used for questions and answers. For instance, choose famous people from the American revolution, or do a series on our first presidents, or famous artists and composers. You may want to choose the questions yourself and let each pair look up the answers. Encourage them to use the information but to make the character personable and to answer in a way that will give us a glimpse of that person's life. When put in this fun and creative format, your students will easily retain more information.

Abraham Lincoln

Leonardo Da Vinci

Mona Lisa

Albert Einstein

Eleanor Roosevelt

Cleopatra

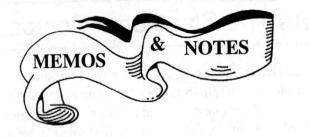

The use of Commercials provide a variety of learning experiences. Everyone is familiar with commercials and that makes them an excellent learning tool. Use these exercises separately or in their natural progression. This can be a single class project using spontaneous creativity; or, it can be spread out over a series of classes allowing for prep time.

OPTIONAL: Ask a parent or a friend to bring in a Video Camera to record each commercial and a T.V. for viewing. This exercise is equally effective without the video camera, but passing the video around to other classrooms is inspiring for both the actors and the viewers, and doesn't require a lot of scheduling..

ITEMS NEEDED: Pencils and Paper. Any necessary props. (Chairs, Hats, Cereal Boxes, etc..)

A) Write a Commercial like one you have heard on T.V., about a common product. Commercials should be from 15 seconds to a maximum of one minute.
EXAMPLES: Tennis shoes, dolls, jeans, insurance, fruit juices, etc..

B) Write a Commercial on an imaginary product.
EXAMPLES: Magic tooth powder, Flying tennis shoes, Rocket trips to the moon, Peanut butter and bologna ice cream, Happy pills, etc.

C) Write a socially conscious commercial or one about a local business.
EXAMPLES: Clean water, Air quality, Clear cutting of trees, Ozone, etc. Or, Volunteering, Adoption, Donating to the poor, Save-A-Pet or Pick a local business that you are familiar with.

D) Another option for a beginning exercise in this series that does require time on the teachers part is to write a series of commercials and assign them to the participants. You can use commercials right off the T.V. Or, you can use the same commercial for each participant, encouraging individuality, finding how many ways there are to accomplish the same thing. Video taping the "test" commercial of its kind gives actors and audience a chance to review the techniques that are the most convincing.

E) All of these commercials can be done solo or with two participants or more. Try it in different ways.

KEY WORDS: **SELL IT! BE CONVINCING! BE ARTISTIC!**

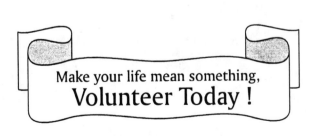

Make your life mean something,
Volunteer Today !

DEATH AND DYING

We are all amateurs at dying, thank God. But as actors and actresses we will die a thousand deaths and each time we must be convincing. Following are a few exercises that will explore and test one of life's greatest mysteries.

I must stress at this point that the subject of suicide should be avoided. People have enough ideas about suicide without our input. It is not something to teach to children in any classroom. So by making a simple rule that none of the games will involve suicide we avoid a sticky subject.

Pick A Death | 90

This is a very popular game. People love to fake a death, especially kids.

Each participant takes a turn to go to the center of the circle or onto the stage. Each chooses a death and then portrays it in front of the group, ending frozen on the floor.

EXAMPLE DEATHS: Gunshot, Bomb in pocket or briefcase, Driving accident, poison, Choking, etc.

ASSIGNMENT:
1) **Decide on a death.**
2) **Go to center of stage or circle.**
3) **Show us something before the death.**
4) **Show us the death.**
5) **Freeze.**

Screamer | 91

Get the group into a wide circle, holding hands. Pass the pulse but this time pass it both directions at once. Say, "Now" as you do it so that people are ready. The object is for one person to receive both pulses at the same time. The receiver must then let out a blood curdling scream and fall to the center of the circle and die the death of his/her choice. Each receiver must remain dead until the last person has fallen; they all must remain perfectly still in the same position and not talk. Keep passing the pulse, both hands at once, picking various players to begin it. You may want to pick players so that the double pulse will avoid you; you can continue leading the game, at least for the first time. You will soon have a pile of dead bodies as your circle grows smaller and smaller until you can barely hold hands. At this point you can call for a mass death by the remaining participants.

NO CONTACT STAGE COMBAT

There are many forms of stage fighting and dueling. If properly executed, stage fighting can be extremely effective and completely safe. It is very important that the director/teacher supervise at all times. It is also important to build a solid base of instruction to ensure that no one ever gets hurt. In this exercise we will concentrate on hand-to-hand combat. Most boys and men will be very good at this right away since it is, or was, a part of their daily play. Some women/girls will have a natural knack for it as well, but most females will need to learn to commit to each and every move. For all students it will be important to develop the habit of following through and committing completely to every move as in dance. Perhaps stage combat is so effective because it is very much like dance. In fact, when using stage combat onstage it will be important to choreograph each and every move to avoid any accidents. Choreographed stage combat is a beautiful and sometimes powerful sight to see.

I, as an instructor, had little experience in combat whether real or staged. I quickly discovered that the boys in my children's workshops and the men in my adult productions would provide me with a thorough training. I now feel extremely competent in choreographing stage combat. I still use the natural ability and the ideas of my actors and actresses.

It would be impossible to teach stage combat on a page of paper, but I will give you the basics to get you started. The crucial thing to remember in stage combat is to never, never touch unless it is choreographed. For instance, one actor may grasp the other's arm to throw him but only gently letting the other actor make the movement. And that is the whole crux of stage fighting. It is up to the actor taking the punch to create the effect. For instance, if an actor punches another actor he will come within four inches of touching the other actor. The other actor, through his exaggerated physical reaction and the pain on his face, will show the full force of the punch. It depends almost entirely on the actor or actress taking the punch whether it will look real or not. I have seen many instance when the punch was not particularly believable, but because of the reaction of the other actor, it worked.

You, the coach, may want to do a small demonstration to start with, either by yourself with a volunteer, or choose two capable participants. Begin by using hand punches; anybody can punch, maybe not correctly, but it is a beginning. The first actor will throw a punch. The second actor does not know where the first actor will direct his punch and has to be ready to react correctly. Remind the first actor to not touch the second actor and to come no closer than four inches, ever. For instance, if the punch lands in the stomach area, the assaulted actor/actress will probably react by doubling over. Remind them to make each move bigger than life. The punch should be strong and extended as far as possible. The reaction should be a fast and hard collapse, as in a hit to the stomach. Don't worry about sound effects. If they happen naturally, fine, otherwise work on them later. Concentrate on the movements at first. Now, it is the second actor's turn to take the punch and it is time for the first actor to provide a believable reaction. Go back and forth, one actor executing the punch and the other actor reacting appropriately, taking turns and taking their time with it. There is no hurry because it has already been decided who will punch and who will react. When doing a play with any kind of stage fighting, this exercise should be done again and again and used in the choreography process.

There are many styles of combat. Depending upon what your play dictates, you may use this same exercise to introduce the style of combat and to insure safety. Some other forms: Karate, wrestling, boxing, etc.

Bringing in professionals, such as martial arts teachers, can add realism to the imitative gestures teaching techniques that fall just short of the real thing.

Occasionally a script will call for dying in combat. It happens in Shakespeare and a few other places. If you must die onstage, it is far better to do it well or not do it at all. It is imperative that your performance be completely believable. Another way to look at it is that there are many things we would not want to experience in real life but can experience on the stage. Often a person who is generally sweet and easy going can play the most effective evil parts. For such a person, it is not type casting and therefore becomes a true performance. (Of course there are great arguments for type casting. There is a time for both.) It is often a catharsis, a vent for the dark side, which we all have. Effective stage dying can serve the same purpose. It can be a way of experiencing the unknown.

This particular exercise is especially designed for the director who is directing a play or musical with a scene that has death by combat. It is suggested that the entire cast be involved even if only a few of the characters are actually cast. It will make it a better workshop and the actual actors will get more ideas that way. Also it will produce better facial reactions in the other actors from experiencing it themselves. Give an assignment for the actors/actresses to watch movies with combat similar to that being used in your production.

Decide on the forms of combat you want to use and develop: Sword fighting, dueling with pistols, the martial arts, etc. Pick sword fighting, for instance. Get into pairs. Decide who will die first, choose A and B. Let the whole group fight in pairs at one time to stimulate the energy. After A dies then start again and let B die. Call out the moment of death so that you, as the coach, can prolong the fight to a good point. Pick a pair that is doing well and have them perform it for the rest of the group. Then send the pairs off on their own to choreograph an entire fight and the moment of death. Each pair should work out their scene alone and come back to perform for the group. After each pair's performance, let the whole group give comments on how to make it better. After every pair has performed, send them back to work alone, incorporating the group's comments to make it better and more realistic. Then switch and let the other actor/actress perform the death to a completely new and different choreography.

Try this exercise with various combat forms. Or, even from the beginning, if you are not performing a particular combat for a particular time piece, let the pairs choose their own combat.

CREATIVE AUDITIONING

We all know that most auditions can be pretty intimidating. Well, since I hold auditions at least five times a year, I have given this subject a lot of thought. I personally don't audition very well. I've done very well at some auditions, but as a whole I don't like the process; and furthermore, I find the experience to be very ineffective. Put me in front of an audience and I have no trouble; I have complete command and never miss a beat. The problem is, you'd never know it from my audition. On the other hand, I have auditioned people who are exceptional at the audition. They read well; they have tremendous energy and respond to the competition. But, they never quite reach that same level in performance. Of course there are people who fall everywhere in between.

It is true that people need to be trained to audition, but most of us are dealing with community theatre. Here, people who audition for you will not be trained and you want to see them at their best. One basic problem is that many people, whether they are adults or children, do not read very well. Also, think about it, we never expect people to go up on the stage in a real performance without any preparation. What an absurd thought! So why should we expect miracles at the audition? As a director, I personally want to see people at their best, not what they can do under the unreal pressure of an audition. I have found that just about anyone who has the proper amount of preparation can give a respectable performance.

I prefer auditions that include prepared works, like monologues. This gives the director a chance to see what the actor/actress can do with some preparation. We don't usually expect a singer to do a cold singing, so why should we expect an actor/actress to do a cold reading? There is a time and place for everything, even cold readings, but the majority of people will not respond well to cold readings.

Cold Readings | 94

Following are some suggestions and ideas for you to incorporate into your audition process. Sometimes there is no avoiding a cold reading. This is a technique that I use:

1) **I make copies of the scenes I want read.**
2) **I assign auditioners into groups of two or three and send them off to work on a scene together.**
3) **I give them time to read the material and think about the character, including time to work out some physical bits, such as: a special accent, or way of walking, or facial feature.**

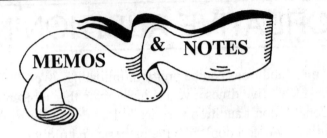

MEMOS & NOTES

Even if a child reads well, he/she often has trouble reading and putting the emotion into the words. I don't even attempt to do any readings whatsoever when it comes to auditioning children. It is important to mention here that reading skills have absolutely nothing to do with acting. Sure it's nice if they can read, but some of my best leads could not read or had poor reading skills. I soon found ways of working around it. I ask the parents to help them learn their lines. I suggest that the parents make a tape, reading all the parts themselves so that the child can listen to it over and over again. I suggest that anyone make a tape. It is my best tool when I am learning lines. On page 149, there is a small section on making tapes as a means of learning lines.

When I audition children, I use several techniques and games. The first thing I do is play a warm up game, usually the freeze-walk. This gets them playing and having fun immediately, letting me see what they can really do. The next thing is to pick one of my quick performing games. For instance, "You Got It/ I Got It," "Getting the Laughs," "Improvisations," any game that can produce a quick performance.

Then I pick out people that I think would do well in certain parts or open it up to whoever would like to try for those parts and have them stand onstage in a line. I then read to them a line from that character in the voice of that character. Then going down the line, they each say that line with as much energy and inflection as they can. I usually do several lines per character, giving everyone plenty of chances. I have gotten great auditions from this technique. I can really narrow down the possibilities. I encourage everyone to try out for everything. How can they know unless they try? How can you as the director know unless they try? There are so many ways to cast a show, and with children there is a tremendous amount of versatility. I go strictly by who is the best for the part. It does not matter if a child is new to theatre or if they have been in my program for four years. If they are right for the part, and have enough talent to pull it off, they get the part. Of course, it often happens that the children who have been in my program for some time, and are trained, have what it takes. I was pleasantly surprised this year when three new participants took three of the leads in our production of "The Magic Flute."

MEMOS & NOTES

Sometimes directors treat their entire audition like a workshop, whether they are auditioning adults or children. The workshop atmosphere insures that you will see all of the participants in some of their best moments. It will give you the opportunity to see how they will take direction. It is a great time to do some in-depth work. Why waste time? Start building your foundation for the play or musical at the audition.

You will want to select activities and exercises that will show you what you need to see for this particular production. For instance, if this is a show that has animal characters, you will want to do an exercise that will show you who can cut loose enough to imitate an animal. This format of auditioning not only shows you actors and actresses at their best, but gives you a jump start for building your foundation. It gives you that valuable extra training time. If you have three days of auditions, it gives you three opportunities to work on character building. Also, you will receive a tremendous number of ideas for the characters, and the blocking, from the auditioners themselves.

A great exercise to use here is in the; "Tell us the story of the up-coming production," on page 86. It will give everyone a view of the goal they are headed towards and even though all the auditioners will not be in the production, the people who are chosen will get that head start and the people not chosen will get a free workshop.

MEMOS & NOTES

EXTRA THEATRE ASSIGNMENTS

Attending The Theatre | 97

One of the best ways to learn about theatre is to go to live theatre productions. Within the time period of working with your group, give them the assignment of going to at least two live theatre productions, either plays or musicals. It is inspiring to see other people up onstage achieving a major goal.

There is nothing like seeing a play to understand the script. It is suggested to anyone thinking of pursuing a career either in professional theatre or in community theatre to see as many shows as possible. Once you have seen a production of that play or musical, you will probably never forget what it is about.

You may want to extend the assignment to include a written report of what they saw. Teach them to find both the positive attributes of the production and the things that can be improved upon.

Reviewing The Production | 98

Tell your participants that they are newspaper critics and have them write a review of a production they have attended. Make sure to tell them to write their reviews with constructive criticism and positive comments. Cut out a few reviews from any newspaper and make copies for the group to read so they can get an idea about what a review should sound like. Teach them that there are always good things about every production and that there is always room for improvement. A good reviewer points out both. Remind them that often critics are overly critical, sometimes trying to establish their own credibility.

Reading The Classics | 99

There is no substitute for reading the classic plays. Either assign the plays to your particular group or let them choose. Reading plays helps us to understand the structure, and exposes us all to classic literature. You may want your group to write a report or a review of what they have read. When possible, a thorough assignment would be to have them read the play and the original book that the play was written from.

A few suggestions for reading are: Shakespeare, Bernard Shaw, "She Stoops to Conquer" by Oliver Goldsmith, "Harvey," "Arsenic and Old Lace," "The Crucible." The list goes on. Encourage them to read plays.

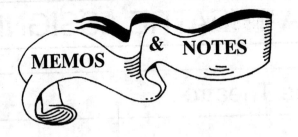

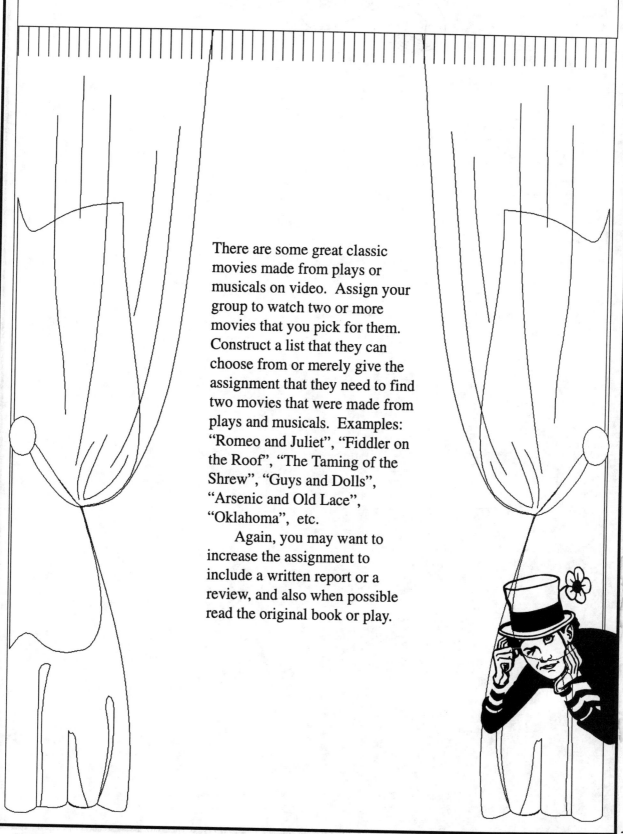

There are some great classic movies made from plays or musicals on video. Assign your group to watch two or more movies that you pick for them. Construct a list that they can choose from or merely give the assignment that they need to find two movies that were made from plays and musicals. Examples: "Romeo and Juliet", "Fiddler on the Roof", "The Taming of the Shrew", "Guys and Dolls", "Arsenic and Old Lace", "Oklahoma", etc.

Again, you may want to increase the assignment to include a written report or a review, and also when possible read the original book or play.

There are many ways to learn and all of us respond differently to various methods. Some people learn best by seeing/reading. There are those who are audio learners, who respond better to sound. It is suggested that actors use every method available to learn lines. The combination of audio and visual is most effective. Of course, the number one tip in learning lines is, start today! Don't wait! Don't procrastinate! It will take the same amount of time later as it will now. Besides, the longer you know your lines, the more you can do with them.

VISUAL LEARNING: Start by reading the play through about ten times. By doing this you will thoroughly understand your material. The most important research you can do is to know the entire play. Then when you begin learning your lines, they will come faster from familiarization. This will also help you get a head start on memorizing your cue lines.

Next, write out different sections of lines on small cards. Wherever you go, take a card or two so that you can be learning a line or two in your spare moments while riding the bus, waiting in a doctor's office, etc. Use cards for lines that you are having trouble with.

Once you know your lines, write or type out all your cue lines then read them aloud and say your own lines from memory. This method is most effective to sharpen your delivery and quicken your timing.

AUDIBLE LEARNING: Make two tapes. First, make a tape reading both your cue lines and your own lines. Listen to it all the time: when you're doing chores; exercising; driving; before you go to bed; any chance you get, even five minutes at a time. This method also works with songs.

When you know your lines fairly well, make another tape with only the cue lines, leaving out your own lines. Read a cue line and then mouth your own line with no sound, so that you will have time to say it in the blank spot. Practice with this tape often. Once the show opens, you can use it as a warm up.

GETTING HELP: Get a friend to read the other parts for you so that you can practice with a real voice.

CHARACTERS

GARBAGE PERSONNEL	BAG LADIES	MOTHERS
LAWYERS	STREET PEOPLE	PREGNANT
JUDGES	BUS DRIVER	FATHERS
JAILBIRDS	SECRETARIES	PARENTS
THE BOSS	STREET SWEEPERS	NURSES
DOCTORS	CHIMNEY SWEEPS	BABIES
ACTRESS	STREET MIME	TEACHERS
MONKEYS	ATHLETES	YOUNG CHILD
BALLERINA	TAP DANCER	ELDERLY PERSON
CARPENTERS	PRINCIPAL	GRANDPARENTS
MOVIE DIRECTOR	ROCK STAR	SIBLINGS
FRUIT PICKERS	COOK	MAID
BUTLER	PRINCESS	PRINCE
KING	QUEEN	CLOWN
ANIMALS	NERDS	TEENAGERS
ARTIST	WINDOW WASHER	DOG WALKER
MODEL	CASHIER	SUN BATHER
JOGGER	BUSINESS PERSON	COACH
NEWSPAPER BOY	GANGSTER	PREACHER
LIFEGUARD	PHOTOGRAPHER	BLIND PERSON

IDEA SHEET

EXAMPLES OF SITUATIONS FOR IMPROVISATION

JOB INTERVIEW	TEACHER/STUDENT	TEACHER/PARENT
PRINCIPAL/STUDENT	PRINCIPAL/TEACHER	PARENT/CHILD
BUMS	BAG LADIES	GANGSTERS
DINNER	PHOTOGRAPHY SESSION	STEWARD/PASSENGER
COOKING SESSION	RESCUE	DANCE CLASS
AT THE MOVIES	RADIO SHOW/INTERVIEW	PHONE CONVERSATION
AT THE ZOO	SOMETHING LOST	AT DISNEYLAND
TOUR	REVEALING A SECRET	AUDITION
GARDENING	ANY JOB SITUATION	PHONE OPERATORS

EMOTIONS

HAPPINESS	ANGER	FRUSTRATION	DEPRESSION
ANXIETY	SADNESS	EXUBERANCE	CONTENTMENT
EXCITED	SCARED	DISGUSTED	CONFIDENT

WEATHER CONDITIONS

COLD	HOT	ICY	SNOWY
HAIL	WARM	MILD	TORNADO
WINDY	PERFECT	HURRICANE	BLIZZARD
RAINY	DRIZZLY	FOGGY	Etc.

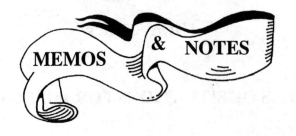

MEMOS & NOTES

MILA AT A GLANCE

Mila Johansen was born with the last name of Grimm in in Santa Monica, California. Her true ancestry traces k to the family tree of the Brothers Grimm of Germany. may very well be these roots that give Mila the instincts and finesse which enable her to write classics into plays and musicals.

Mila has every play catalogue available in print sitting on her book shelf. Still, she has had a hard time finding suitable material to be performed in her workshops. As a result, she has written twelve plays and musicals that have all been produced with great success. She has created a unique and timely catalogue of plays called, "Classics With A Twist". Mila figured that if she couldn't find well written plays conducive to casts of thirty or more, than perhaps other teachers and directors were having the same problem. "Classics With A Twist" is now filling that void throughout the U.S. and internationally.

Mila Johansen has taught children's theatre for the past twelve years with acclaimed success. Over the years, she has developed a series of games that are specifically designed to bring out the natural talent in both children and adults while teaching them theatre etiquette and technique. Mila has directed more than sixty plays and musicals with both children and adult casts. She is the founder of the Nevada County Performing Arts Guild, a community theatre production company that is entering it's eleventh year.

Mila in 1955

"My daughter and I have had the pleasure of working under the direction of Mila Johansen over the past four seasons. I enthusiastically recommend these theatre exercises and games as enhancers of creativity, expression and self-esteem."

Eric M. Rubinstein, M.D.
Diplomate, American Board of Psychiatry & Neurology

"Mila's theatre games are a wonderful classroom tool which a teacher can use to promote an attitude of mutual support and respect among children--freeing each to use his/her imagination in ways incorporating both mind and body. Such freedom to risk is a rare opportunity in our competitive society."

Gail Lipson, Classroom Teacher
M.S. Early childhood Education